Creating Excellence

Creating Excellence

Becoming an A+ School

Vernon G. Smith

ROWMAN & LITTLEFIELD
Lanham • Boulder • New York • London

Published by Rowman & Littlefield
A wholly owned subsidiary of The Rowman & Littlefield Publishing Group, Inc.
4501 Forbes Boulevard, Suite 200, Lanham, Maryland 20706
www.rowman.com

Unit A, Whitacre Mews, 26–34 Stannary Street, London SE11 4AB

Copyright © 2018 by Vernon G. Smith

All rights reserved. No part of this book may be reproduced in any form or by any electronic or mechanical means, including information storage and retrieval systems, without written permission from the publisher, except by a reviewer who may quote passages in a review.

British Library Cataloguing in Publication Information Available

Library of Congress Cataloging-in-Publication Data
ISBN: 978-1-4758-1433-0 (cloth : alk. paper)
ISBN: 978-1-4758-1434-7 (pbk. : alk. paper)
ISBN: 978-1-4758-1435-4 (electronic)

∞™ The paper used in this publication meets the minimum requirements of American National Standard for Information Sciences—Permanence of Paper for Printed Library Materials, ANSI/NISO Z39.48–1992.

Printed in the United States of America

Contents

Preface		vii
Acknowledgments		xi
1	Change and the Demands on Education	1
2	Philosophy of Education	5
	Why Address Philosophy of Education	5
	Need for a School Philosophy	6
	Leaders and Self-Examination	9
	Developing the School's Philosophy of Education	11
	Philosophical Thought for Consideration	15
	Sample School Philosophy of Education Statement	16
3	The Vision	21
	What Is Vision?	21
	Why School Vision	22
	Leadership Role in Visioning	24
	The Process	25
4	Climate and Culture	35
	What Is School Climate?	35
	The Importance of Climate	39
	The Desired Climate	41
	Role of the Principal	46
	What Is School Culture?	47
	The Principal's Role	49

5	Recruitment and Development of Staff	55
	Recruitment and Selection	55
	Classroom Observations	59
	Professional Development	62
6	Rigor and High Expectations	67
	Why the Need for Rigor	67
	What Is Rigor?	69
	High Expectations and Rigor	76
	Higher-Order Thinking and Rigor	78
	Gallagher & Aschner Classification Model	79
	Gallagher & Aschner Classification Scheme	80
	Recommendations for the Practicing Principal	81
	Creating Rigor in the Classroom	82
	Message for the Educational Leader	92
7	Engaging Parents for School Success	99
	The Importance of Parental Support and Involvement	100
	Ways to Involve and Empower Parents	103
	The Need for a School-Community Relations Plan	105
	Conclusion	112
8	Persistence and Drive—Never Give Up!	115
	Union Negotiations	116
	Understanding Resistance to Change	119
	Anticipate Areas of Resistance	119
	Dealing with Difficult Teachers	122
	Dealing with Unruly Parents	129
	Converting Unwilling Students	133
	Be the Change You Want to See	136

About the Author   141

Preface

As Coordinator of the Master of Science in Educational Leadership Program at Indiana University Northwest, I frequently and repeatedly ask program candidates, "What do you want and how badly do you want it?" Before becoming a full-time professor, I served as a building principal for twenty years. As a teacher, I applied for an administrative position in the school corporation where I taught. I had garnered reputation as a top teacher and won teaching awards. However, I had the baggage of also being a local elected official. Therefore, my candidacy for an administrative position fueled much controversy and doubt with the superintendent and some school board members. I got a position, and I set out to prove all the naysayers wrong. I wanted my school to demonstrate academic excellence, and I wanted it badly.

At each school where I served as a principal, I worked hard, overtime, shepherded the school's vision, used best practices, demonstrated and required high expectations, involved all stakeholders, created a wholesome and stimulating climate for learning, and led the faculty and staff in using data-driven instruction. Ultimately, I provided the leadership to create a learning community in the quest for excellence at each of the schools. My last principal position was at an inner-city school. When I inherited the school, it was ranked among the twenty-eight elementary schools in the district as twenty-third in math and seventeenth in reading. Seven years later it was ranked seventh in both areas. I was gaining excellence for my school and achieving it because I wanted it badly.

Today educational leaders have a more overwhelming challenge to ensure that all students regardless of race and economic status are career - and college ready. The job is greater than the school alone; all stakeholders must accept responsibility and play a part in achieving academic success. However, leadership for improving teaching and learning must come foremost from the principal and other educational leaders. Ron Edmonds, known as the father of effective school research, made a cogent statement about effective schooling. He said, "We can, whenever and wherever we choose, successfully teach all children whose schooling is of interest to us. We already know more than we need to do that. Whether or not we do it must finally depend on how we feel about the fact that we haven't so far." The question is: What do you want and how badly do you want it? If you desire academic excellence, this book has been written to share the knowledge base, impart the technical skills, and highlight the interpersonal skills recommended to enable you to create excellence and enable your school to become an A+ school. The book is based on focus areas and the actions and tools I found productive and that helped me to provide leadership in improving the academic performance in the schools I led.

Creating Excellence: Becoming an A+ School is intended to be used by first-year principals who have inherited a school that is failing or not achieving to a desired level, as well as by seasoned principals who are struggling to improve their school's academic performance. It can also be used effectively as a textbook for graduate students preparing for a career in educational leadership.

The book is straightforward in its presentation of practices and strategies supported by research and theory. Within the chapters, tools, techniques, and concrete examples are offered. Educational leaders are encouraged to select, revise, and adjust proposed actions based on their own judgment and according to their local conditions, faculty, staff, and other stakeholders. Regardless, improving instruction in order to increase student learning must be the focus.

In the field, we so often hear about practitioners who verbally express defeatism or demonstrate the same in their behavior. In actuality, they have become survivors aiming to preserve their position until they can find another position or retire. Often, they are floating in status quo cesspools. This book devotes a chapter challenging neophytes, seasoned practitioners, and aspiring candidates not to give up, noting that the battle is not over until you quit. Effective educational leaders do not die on the job. Effective educational leaders are persistent, resilient, creative, and committed. They believe, as author Eric Thomas reminds us in his book *The Secret of Success,* that a setback is a setup for a comeback.

Also, key is involving all stakeholders in the quest for academic excellence. The book devotes one chapter to parental engagement. During the first generation of effective schools' research Edmonds and Lezotte identified five correlates of effective schools. In the second generation of effective schools' research, Lezotte identified seven correlates adding positive home–school relations. He makes two salient points: leaders of effective schools use a variety of strategies to provide opportunities and motivate parents and caregivers to be involved with their children's schooling in order to create a strong partnership that makes student success more possible, and leaders of effective schools create a school climate that nurtures a genuine partnership between teachers and parents and cultivates a learning community where all stakeholders have the same goal: a quality education and a successful future for every child. We get more touchdowns if all the players know and are committed to the plan. This book is written for educational leaders who desire to mobilize their own communities to support student success. It provides vivid, concrete illustrations of what can be done based on real experiences and shares other promising ideas worth trying. All stakeholders must want excellence, and it is the educational leader's responsibility to motivate all stakeholders to want it "badly."

Acknowledgments

To God, the head of my life, from whom all blessings flow.

In memory of my mother, Rev. Julia E. Smith, who sacrificed for me, inspired and motivated me, supported my educational pursuits, and, most of all, introduced me to God—all of which made me what I am today.

In appreciation to one of my colleagues, Dr. Shelia Marie Trzcinka, who gave unselfishly of her time to critique and advise me on the contents of this book. I cherish her friendship and constant support.

In appreciation to another one of my colleagues, Timothy (Tim) Sutherland, who gave unselfishly of his time to help me with my references.

Chapter 1

Change and the Demands on Education

A portion of the lyrics of a popular song, "Everything Must Change," written by Benard Ighner states:

> Everything must change
> Nothing stays the same
> Everyone will change
> No one stays the same
> The young become the old
> And mysteries do unfold
> Cause that's the way of time
> Nothing and no one goes unchanged

This portion of the lyric in a unique way expresses the belief that nothing or no one stays the same. Change is constant. We may not be aware of the changes, but change is occurring. There are no static places in time. One is either progressing or regressing, knowingly or unknowingly. Kehoe (2008) states that there is a law of change that is constantly affecting our lives that we are often reluctant to acknowledge. Just as Rip Van Winkle slept through the American Revolution, too many of us as educators may have been asleep and unconscious of the societal changes that have occurred that have affected and impacted public education.

Kehoe argues that change happens everywhere with everyone constantly and it is the one constant of which we can be absolutely sure. Note that there are two primary causes of change: dissatisfaction and agitation. Dissatisfaction, which is an internal force, leads us to change our hairstyle, lose or gain weight, alter our style of dress, and so on. Likewise, dissatisfaction leads us as educators to change the way we instruct, select alternate methods of discipline, and explore and utilize more effective ways of relating to our students. When we are not pleased with the results, we decide to change our approaches. On the other hand, agitation caused by an external force motivates, even drives, us to change.

Choice, of course, is a major factor with internal dissatisfaction or with external pressure or agitation; people have the choice of deciding whether or not to change. However, with agitation there are more direct consequences to resisting change. If we chose not to change or are not competent enough to meet the demand of the change, we suffer the consequences. As children when we disobeyed and our parents or guardians wanted us to change our behavior and we chose not to, we were punished. Likewise, as adults, society has ways of punishing resistors. No Child Left Behind, a federal enactment, legislation passed by state legislatures and policies passed by state boards of education demand change. When we as educators resist or fail to meet the requirements, the result is termination, loss of a position, or state takeover.

Those among us who are alert and perceive the forest and are not just focusing on the trees have known that in recent decades many forces in society have become increasingly dissatisfied with public education. Unfortunately, too many of us did not respond, and those of us who did were not effective enough. We did not tell our story. Our schools were not as bad as they were being portrayed, and we failed to fight rumors with facts. We remained docile, complaining among ourselves.

We did not become a Ron Edmonds, who responded diligently to James Coleman's Equality of Educational Opportunity Report of 1966. That report, which described certain aspects of our educational system and related them to educational achievement, concluded that public schools do not make a significant difference; it was the student's family background that was the main determiner of student success in schools. His findings proposed that children living in poverty, lacking the fundamental conditions or values to support education, could not learn, regardless of what the school did.

In response, Edmonds pioneered the idea that *all students can learn,* not just be allowed into classrooms, but actually learn there in spite of disadvantaged backgrounds and other issues. Studying schools with students of color and others living in poverty, Edmonds identified conditions he termed "effective school correlates" that were present in schools that successfully educate children of poverty. His work led to the Effective Schools Movement that grew in the United States and ultimately globally replaced a vision of despair with a vision of hope for many students in most large cities and rural districts. He was emphatic that student performance does not derive from family background but instead from school response to family background.

Over the decades we have had a choice to respond, to make necessary changes, and if not, to defend what we were doing. Certainly over the recent past there were valid criticisms of schools, maybe not in a blanket fashion, but of individual or groups of schools. It is sad, even tragic, that we collectively did not get internally dissatisfied and make the necessary changes. Because of our lack or inadequacy of response, multiple legislatures, filled with noneducators stimulated by the media that is too accountability-driven and focused on evaluation of schools, rather than the students—students who need remediation—are coming up with "quick fixes" for public education.

Some educators have decided that they are not going to change, but since we cannot control others and control the variables, changes are still occurring. Society has changed and is changing, families have changed and are changing, and children have changed and are changing. Legislation is growing that places more demands on educators, detailing in an unprecedented way expectations of schools and school practitioners, creating more competitors for dwindling dollars allocated for public education. Still we have a choice. Kehoe (2008) notes:

> Working with the dynamics of choice means embracing change as a constant reality in our life, being vigilant in looking for changes that would help us, and then being proactive in initiating them. In business there is an old maxim that says that no business stays the same year after year. You are either gaining market share or losing market share. You are either innovating new products and gaining on your competition or your competition is innovating new products and gaining on you. You are becoming either more competitive or less competitive. You are either gaining customers or losing customers. If things are going well you may choose to make no changes and run your business exactly as you have in the past. The marketplace, however, is not static. It is a constant hive of activity and change, and by not initiating change you may easily fall behind. We usually don't make changes when things are going well, but we must pay homage to the Change Gods; they demand change, and if we do not initiate change, life will initiate it for us. (p. 1)

Schools are expected to engage in continuous renewal, and change expectations are constantly torpedoed their way. Whether we realize it or not, if we can't be on the forefront of change, we must manage change. It is the key to every successful entity, business, school, home, church, and others. Responding to the constant nature of change, we need to assess and plan. Assessing is determining where we have been and where we are now. Planning is determining where we want to go and how we will get there. Through analysis and discussion, we need to determine what we will keep and what we will alter.

Change is not always about the larger, more visual aspects of planning (goals and objectives), but the things that might need to be changed may be the smaller elements of planning (strategies and tactics). Addressing change requires vision, commitment, and passion. Adding more hours to the day, spending more dollars, raising standards, securing better talent to the team, and other "quick fixes" will not do it in themselves. The going has gotten tough, and without vision, commitment, and passion the successful change continuum will be broken.

With the constant chattering for changes in our public schools, leaders, especially building principals, are key. The principal and his or her leadership team have to be the champions of the change. They must recognize that schools do not change until the stakeholders do. Leaders must become real change agents. Those skilled in change understand and appreciate its volatile character, and they purposely seek ideas for coping with and influencing change toward the desired end(s).

Principals must utilize strategies that often call for a shift in the attitude of stakeholders, modified behavior, the acquisition of new skills, and increased determination. They are responsible for building and nurturing a climate for change, one that can be built on and further developed. They are responsible for developing the need for change, unfreezing old behaviors and, through use of various professional development strategies, initiating the change. They are responsible for monitoring the change process and making modifications and revisions, if necessary, until the change is institutionalized.

At the center and heart of continuous improvement are the people who make up a school, the stakeholders. The principal and the leadership team must work to ensure that all stakeholders buy into the change, are committed to the change, are willing to review what they are doing, and, if necessary, make the necessary revisions with an ultimate desire to help students improve academically. Changes need to be made within classrooms and buildings with district support in order for students to begin achieving at a higher and desired level. Finally, we must recognize that the desired change will not occur overnight, but with commitment and effective planning, improvement will happen. Kehoe (2008) concludes:

> So too in our lives, change is the one constant that we can be absolutely sure of. So why don't we live our lives acknowledging this and initiate change on a regular basis, thus putting ourselves in harmony and rhythm with this process? Why is change so hard to embrace? We must learn to be comfortable with change and eventually embrace it. The Mind Power practitioner works with the law of change, initiating changes through choice, will and practice. Initiating change while flowing with the changes as they happen, is a dance with life that the Mind Power practitioner loves to do. (p. 1)

REFERENCE

Kehoe, J. (2008). *Nature of reality & consciousness: The law of change.* Retrieved October, 8, 2014, from http://www.learnmindpower.comjarticlesjthe-law-of/

Chapter 2

Philosophy of Education

WHY ADDRESS PHILOSOPHY OF EDUCATION

The impact of a philosophy of education for a school cannot be overstated. Nolan and Hoover (2008) indicate that authenticity and clarity in espousing a particular educational philosophy are important ingredients in effective teaching. Witcher, Sewall, Arnold, and Travers (2001) note that there will always be a set of beliefs and values (implicit or explicit) that guide teachers' practice and reflect the teacher's education philosophy in all aspects of the education process. Beswick (2005) points out that a teacher's personal philosophy plays a central role in the development of teaching practice.

Although stated two decades ago, the words of Kagan (1992) are worthy of our attention and are just as applicable today as when they were first stated. She said, "As we learn more about the forms and functions of teacher belief, we are likely to come a great deal closer to understanding how effective teachers are made" (p. 85). Noting that effective instruction depends on school and teacher instructional goals, Glickman, Gordon, and Ross-Gordon (2010) state:

> Instructional goals, in turn, are ultimately based on beliefs concerning such things as the purpose of education, what should be taught, the nature of the learner, and the learning process. Whether or not we are conscious of it, teachers' and supervisors' educational philosophies have a significant impact on instruction and instructional improvement efforts. (p. 93)

Often when we think of philosophies of education we think of an individual's philosophy of education. We forget that a school is the sum total of its parts, so it is just as important to ask what is a school's philosophy of education. Within the past two decades, attention to a school establishing a philosophy of education has faded into the background of educational discussions. In spite of the fact that beliefs play such an important role, they have not received much attention from researchers. Bredo (2002) suggests that research on teacher beliefs, attitudes, and values has been ignored or minimally acknowledged. Kagan in her research on teacher beliefs and their impact on teaching supports this view. Nespor (1987) has remarked that we know very little about how beliefs come into being, how they are supported or weakened, how people are converted to them. He notes:

> However, in spite of arguments that people's beliefs are important influences on the ways they conceptualize tasks and learn from experience, relatively little attention has been accorded to the structures and functions of teachers' beliefs about their roles, their students, the subject matter areas they teach, and the schools they work in. (p. 317)

The hot topics today appear to be accountability and student achievement. Legislators and other policy makers in this age of increased accountability and test craziness fail to understand the significance of a school's philosophy of education and how it impacts academic achievement. A healthy, strong philosophy of education enhances the capacity of teachers and students in a variety of settings to create or transform a school's culture. Therefore, it is illogical to attempt to develop a school of academic excellence without focusing on that school's philosophy of education.

NEED FOR A SCHOOL PHILOSOPHY

A school's philosophy of education blossoms from the belief systems of the stakeholders. Obviously, few would deny that there is a link to what one believes or thinks to how one acts. A philosophy of education reflects one's approach to education. Glickman, Gordon, and Ross-Gordon (2005) state "many educators view discussions of educational philosophy as overly abstract and irrelevant to the real world of supervisors and teachers" (p. 96). However, every action of supervisors, teachers, paraprofessionals, and other staff members is based on beliefs, which in turn reflect a broader educational philosophy of the school.

As educators, we often talk about the affective, cognitive, and psychomotor domains, but we fail to understand the connectedness of the three domains. It is what one values (affective) that determines what one believes (cognitive) and ultimately determines one's actions (psychomotor). The connectedness of the three domains is so intertwined that one acts almost spontaneously with little or no forethought. With this in mind, if a school is to be effective, the school's philosophy of education must be explored and given painstaking consideration.

A school's philosophy of education is the collection of individual philosophies of education held by internal stakeholders, which becomes the foundation, knowingly or unknowingly, for a school. It may become not only a major factor, but also the key or sole determiner of whether or not a school is successful in becoming effective in educating all of its students. While individuality is to be valued and not stifled, it is unsound, unproductive, and even dangerous for each teacher and staff member to have an isolated philosophy of education that may not blend together for the good of students. Palmer (1998) notes, "We teach who we are" (p. 2). Trigwell and Prosser (1997) add:

> The individual and the world are not constituted independently of one another. Individuals and the world are internally related through the individuals' awareness of the world. Mind does not exist independently of the world around it. The world is an experienced world. (p. 2)

Pajares (1992) provides a synthesis of the findings on beliefs that he drew from his review of the literature on the topic that supports and underscores Palmer's view that "we teach who we are":

1. Beliefs are formed early and tend to self-perpetuate, persevering even against contradiction caused by reason, time, schooling, or experience.
2. Individuals develop a belief system that houses all the beliefs acquired through the process of cultural transmission.
3. The belief system has an adaptive function in helping individual define and understand the world and themselves.
4. Knowledge and beliefs are inextricably intertwined, but the potent affective, evaluative, and episodic nature of beliefs makes them a filter through which new phenomenon are interpreted.
5. Thought processes may well be precursors to and creators of beliefs, but the filtering effect of belief structures ultimately screens, redefines, distorts, or reshapes subsequent thinking and information processing.
6. Epistemological beliefs play a key role in knowledge interpretation and cognitive monitoring.
7. Beliefs are prioritized according to their connections or relationship to other beliefs or other cognitive and affective structures. Apparent inconsistencies may be explained by exploring the functional connections and centrality of the beliefs.
8. Belief substructures, such as educational beliefs, must be understood in terms of their connections not only to each other but also to other, perhaps more central, beliefs in the system. Psychologists usually refer to these substructures as attitudes and values.

9. By their very nature and origin, some beliefs are more incontrovertible than others.
10. The earlier a belief is incorporated into the belief structure, the more difficult it is to alter. Newly acquired beliefs are most vulnerable to change.
11. Belief change during adulthood is a relatively rare phenomenon, the most common cause being a conversion from one authority to another or a gestalt shift. Individuals tend to hold on to beliefs based on incorrect or incomplete knowledge even after scientifically correct explanations are presented to them.
12. Beliefs are instrumental in defining tasks and selecting the cognitive tools with which to interpret, plan, and make decisions regarding such tasks; hence, they play a critical role in defining behaviour and organizing knowledge and information.
13. Beliefs strongly influence perception, but they can be an unreliable guide to the nature of reality.
14. Individuals' beliefs strongly affect their behavior.
15. Beliefs must be inferred and this inference must take into account the congruence among individuals' belief statements, the intentionality to behave in a predisposed manner, and the behavior related to the belief in question.
16. Beliefs about teaching are well established by the time a student gets to college. (p. 324)

Pajares (1992) also provides insight into how beliefs function and how this functioning actually contributes to their resistance to change:

> [beliefs] provide personal meaning and assist in defining relevancy. They help individuals to identify with one another and form groups and social systems. On a social and cultural level, they provide elements of structure, order, direction and shared values. From both a personal and socio/cultural perspective, belief systems reduce dissonance and confusion, even when dissonance is logically justified by the inconsistent beliefs one holds. This is one reason why they acquire emotional dimensions and resist change. People grow comfortable with their beliefs, and these beliefs become their "self" so that individuals come to be identified and understood by the very nature of the beliefs, the habits they own. (p. 317)

Some philosophers believe that individuals are the sum total of their experiences. Truthfully, we know that all of our experiences are not good and may cause us to possess negative views, become biased, closed-minded, and subjective. With this in mind, consider the position that every individual in an organization adds to or subtracts from the quality of the organization;

thus, since the school is an organization, each individual adds to or subtracts from the effectiveness of a school. Biased and negative beliefs held by internal stakeholders must be unfrozen and supplanted with more positive views. Even limited educational experience will reveal that among educators there is a dichotomy of thought concerning the education of our young: liberal versus vocational education, education for personal development or education for citizenship, education versus enculturation, teaching versus educating, training versus indoctrination, levels of classroom control, rights of children, rights of parents, and so on. There is much to be gained by shedding light upon these issues and in promoting reflection or discussion on them by stakeholders with a goal of creating a consensus of thought that will lead to effective instruction.

While diversity is to be valued, too much diversity (negative or positive philosophies) may negatively impact the effectiveness of the school. Sergiovanni and Starratt (1983) stress the need for an expressed foundation of principles and add that some have often called unexpressed constellation of principles a platform. They conclude that just as a political party is supposed to base its decisions and actions on a party platform, so too should school personnel have a platform to carry on their work. We know that contractors must lay a foundation in order to build a structure that will not sink. Likewise in education, a school's philosophy of education becomes the base, the foundation for any plan, program, or activity.

LEADERS AND SELF-EXAMINATION

Sergiovanni and Starratt (1983) note the importance of understanding one's own beliefs, especially those of supervisors. Glickman et al. (2010) point out that most supervisors (school leaders) are former teachers. They add,

> As a result, their views about learning, the nature of the learner, knowledge and the role of the teacher in the classroom influence their view of supervision. After all, supervision is in many respects analogous to teaching. Teachers wish to improve students' behavior, achievement, and attitudes. Supervisors similarly wish to improve teachers' behavior, achievement, and attitudes. (p. 95)

Educational leaders should explore their beliefs because often they may be the source of the problem. In addition to analyzing their views about learning, the nature of the learner and knowledge, and the role of the teacher, they need to reflect on their knowledge base, their interpersonal skills, and their technical skills. Additionally they need to consider their administrative style—autocratic, laissez-faire, democratic/participative, transactional, transformational—as well as their supervisory style—directive, nondirective, or collaborative (Glickman et al., 2010). Tas (2011) notes:

> Studies that cover education management have uncovered a relation between the level of effectiveness of schools and the way they are managed. Familiarity of the school administrator with management theories is important for his/her understanding of school employees' situation and factors behind their behavior. If the administrator manages to understand and grasp the factors leading the employees to behave in one way or another, he/she will be capable of better managing them in consideration of those factors. He/she will then be able to guide the employees to behave in line with the goals of the organization. (p. 568)

Autocratic leaders make decisions alone with little or no input of others. They provide clear expectations of what needs to be done, when it should be done, and how it should be done. Laissez-faire leaders fail to provide direct supervision and regular feedback to subordinates. They provide little or no guidance to the group and leave decision making up to group members. Democratic leaders (also known as participative leaders) value input from team members and peers. They forge consensus through participation but retain the authority to make the final decision.

Transactional leaders, who hold power and control, provide incentives for subordinates to do what they want. If an employee does what is desired, a reward will follow; if not, a punishment will follow. Transformational leaders motivate subordinates; they enhance productivity and efficiency through communication and high visibility. They are able to inspire followers to change expectations, perceptions, and motivations to work toward common goals.

Glickman and Tamashiro (1980) define three supervisory styles as follows:

- Directive supervision is an approach based on belief that teaching consists of technical skill with known standards and competencies for all teachers to be effective. The supervisor's role is to inform, direct, model, assess those competencies.
- Collaborative supervision is based on the belief that teaching is primarily problem solving, whereby two or more persons jointly pose hypotheses to a problem, experiment, and implement those teaching strategies that appear to be most relevant in their own surroundings. The supervisor's role is to guide the problem-solving process, be an active member of the interaction, and keep the teachers focused on their common problems.
- Non-directive supervision has as its premise that learning is primarily a private experience in which individuals must come up with their own solutions to improving the classroom experience for students. The supervisor's

role is to listen, be nonjudgmental, and provide self-awareness and clarification experiences for teachers. (p. 76)

A supervisor or school leader who uses directive supervision sees him/herself as being the expert on instruction and therefore has the major responsibility for decision making. A supervisor or school leader who uses nondirective supervision views the teacher as being capable of instruction improvement and acts as a facilitator in the process. Finally, a supervisor or school leader who uses collaborative supervision considers him/herself as being an equal partner with the teacher in instructional improvement with equal responsibility.

Glickman et al. (2010) note that as school leaders clarify their educational philosophy or supervisory beliefs, they rarely find a pure ideological position, but they will create a synthesized combination that becomes a platform for leadership. They add that a particular platform is neither right nor wrong, rather it is the bits and pieces that have metamorphosed or evolved. The bottom line is that in quest of academic excellence, education leaders need to do some introspect and determine what they believe and if those beliefs are conductive to effective instructions.

DEVELOPING THE SCHOOL'S PHILOSOPHY OF EDUCATION

After reflecting on their beliefs, school leaders should lead their faculty and staff members in discussing what they believe. Zmuda, Kuklis, and Kline (2004) note, "To move from individual autonomy to collective autonomy, stakeholders must engage in collegial conversations about the school, its purpose, its beliefs, and its problems" (p. 62). While many will echo the belief statement that has become popular in educational circles and setting, that is, "all children can learn," it would be fair to conclude that some will have some beliefs that they will feel uncomfortable to share. Educators are made up of the people of society, and they bring to schools the negative beliefs about people and learning based on gender, race, economics, and others. While we may encounter difficulty changing some of our stakeholders' negative beliefs, we must not let them feel comfortable having them.

Educators have a responsibility for what they do in the educational setting of the school, and what they do, consciously or unconsciously, is linked to their belief set, their philosophy of education. While leaders cannot literally control adult behavior, healthy discussions of beliefs and consensus building of a school philosophy of education will move us closer to the quest for academic excellence. Glickman et al. (2010), in discussing cultural background and philosophy, raise an interesting point. They note, "Educators' beliefs about education often are influenced by cultural assumptions that they may not be aware of because the assumptions are so deeply ingrained and taken for granted" (p. 104).

Philosophical discussions will help colleagues develop a sense of common concerns, formulate instructional aims, agree on methodology, and identify mutually acceptable strategies of educating. Needless to say, reconstructing a lost tradition of creating a philosophy of education for schools in an age of reform will yield student performance benefits. School leaders should provide opportunities for philosophical discourse involving stakeholders in open, reflective, intuitive, robust, critical dialogue on questions such as:

What is the purpose of education?
What are the aims of this educational enterprise?
What role do we play in educating our students?
What is the role of the student in education?
What role do parents and the community play in educating our students?
What are the best ways to teach our students?
What are your beliefs on how children learn?
How do we best address the needs of our students?
How do we balance addressing the diverse needs of students while meeting the needs of the entire class?
How can we produce effective teaching and learning?

Figure 2.1 is a philosophy template that was developed by the University of Minnesota for individual use that has been modified for school use.

Another example of a philosophy template that school leaders may use in leading internal stakeholders in developing their school's philosophy of education is offered in figure 2.2.

To be most productive in developing a philosophy of education for a school, school leaders should understand the importance of giving credit to others, respecting others' views including those with whom one disagrees within the philosophical conversation, and ensuring that others' perspectives are heard and valued. It is not just important, but it is vital in building human relationships. When we don't respect others' beliefs, others may interpret that we are not just disrespecting their views, but we are disrespecting them as well.

Every opinion is not valid and sound and could be harmful, so unsound opinions need to be challenged. As leaders, we challenge others' opinions and views; however, we must not leave others feeling morally crushed. Rhetoric, discussion, and persuasion including facts should be used as the means to challenge faulty opinions and views. Use of derogatory language and behavior will not lead to the creation of a collegial faculty and staff. We must aim to treat everyone with the same level of respect, regardless of how obscure

Table 2.1

Teaching Philosophy Template

Areas to address in [our]
Teaching Philosophy:

[Our] aspirations/goals/objectives:
- **as a teacher:**

(i.e., encourage mastery, competency, transformational learning, life-long learning, general skill transference of skills, meaningful learning, critical thinking, etc.)

- **for [our] students:**

(See examples above)
*Describe and give example(s)

What methods will [we] consider to reach these goals/objectives?

(i.e., [our] beliefs regarding learning theory and specific strategies we would use . . . such as case studies, group work, simulations, interactive lectures, learning/reading circles, etc. . . . Include any new ideas/strategies we have used or want to try.

*Describe and give example(s) of strategies/practices that [we] prefer).

How will [we] assess student understanding?

(What are [our] beliefs about grading . . . norm-referenced or criterion-referenced? What different types of assessment will you use . . . . traditional tests? Alternative assessments such as projects, papers, panels, presentation, etc.?)

*Describe and give example(s)

How will [we] improve our teaching?

(i.e., How will [we] use [our] student evaluations to improve [our] teaching? How might [we] learn new skills? How do [we] know when [we] have taught effectively?)

Any examples [we] can share?

Additional considerations:
- Why is teaching important to [us]?
- How do [we] collaborate with others?
- What beliefs, theories, and/or methods mark [our] successful teaching?
- How do [we] maintain positive relationships with [our] students? With colleagues?

Reprinted with the permission of the Center for Educational Innovation, University of Minnesota.

Table 2.2   Philosophy Template

Philosophy Template				
Our vision, mission, goals, and objectives for our school	Methods and best practices we will use to reach our vision, mission, and goals	How will we evaluate student learning and achievement?	How will we improve our teaching?	Are there any additional considerations we want to call attention to?
What is the vision for our school? What is the mission for our school? What do we want to achieve for our students? Consider life long learning, relevant learning, critical thinking, etc.	What are our educational beliefs? What are the best practices to use to achieve our vision? What specific educational strategies will we use in our classrooms? How do we best meet the needs of all students? Will we use case studies, group work, hands-on activities, project-based learning, simulations, interactive lectures, and so on?	How will we grade? What types of assessments will we use? What standardized tests will we use? Will we use outcome learning? What percentages will we attribute to each?	How can we use student formative assessments to improve our teaching? How will we master new skills and improve our instruction? How will we determine if our teaching is effective?	What do we value? How can we be collaborative as a faculty? How can we have the most effective classroom management? What tools of discipline will we use? On what else do we want to focus?

others' beliefs are, colleagues deserve the same opportunity to present those beliefs as others. We must be advocates of tolerance and demonstrators of patience. Doing so builds trust and a climate for change.

Following a full discussion on focus questions, school leaders should work to build a consensus of thought, a broad accepted view, not an individual perspective of a philosophy of education. Consensus building in developing a school's philosophy is important because schools are composed of diverse groups of people with different interests. Like society, today's schools are experiencing many problems. As society addresses its problems, individuals and groups come to rely on each other; they become interdependent. Building a consensus on the philosophy for a school builds not only interdependence but also ownership.

Of course, there will be resistors. A discussion of the need for school success should prelude the beginning of any consensus-building process. While these resistors should not be allowed to be blockers, every effort should be made to meet the interests of the resistors in an effort to unify the combined talents of all in the quest for academic excellence. Consensus building offers a way for individuals and groups to collaborate on solving complex problems in ways that are acceptable to all. The result in this stage of creating an A+ school is the school's philosophy of education, the foundation for the vision.

Philosophical, educational discussions cannot be a one-time experience; they must be held strategically. Bringing about positive educational changes is hard work, but it's doable. It takes commitment from the entire school body to succeed. It requires the maintaining of a focus on instructional excellence. Principals and other school leaders must be in the forefront of all improvement efforts. The agreed-upon philosophy must get into the educational souls of the internal stakeholders. Leaders of the school are responsible to make sure this happens.

Additionally, the perspective of stakeholders with negative mind-sets is broadened by discussions on topics such as trust and respect, caring and motivating, bringing life into a curriculum, stimulating critical thinking, and the purposes of education, among others. The results become the common threads that are the foundation for achieving the vision and setting the course for the mission of the school. Needless to say, the lack of a unified philosophy for education lessens the chance for a school to achieve its vision.

PHILOSOPHICAL THOUGHT FOR CONSIDERATION

In 1961, the Educational Policies Commission took the position that the central purpose of American education was to create thinking individuals. It did not imply this purposeful objective should be the school's sole objective, or that it should be the most important objective in all cases, but that it was worthy of being the highest priority of the school. While the approaches of states vary, most states are requiring standardized testing, and the cry for excellence has transformed state-standardized testing into high-stakes testing (Center for Public Education, 2006). Thinking skills today are measured via many state-mandated tests (Hummel & Huitt, 1994). Students are not held responsible for just the correct answer; they must defend and justify their answers. It seems that states are in agreement that the central purpose of education is to create thinking individuals who have mastered critical thinking skills.

Schools can be effective (Edmonds, 1979) in creating thinking individuals and environments where all children can and will learn. The key to making this become a reality is the people to whom we delegate the educational task. People make organizations, like schools, effective, but people also destroy organizations. Glickman et al. (2005) in their research on characteristics of improving schools list, among other factors, sources of leadership, including teacher leadership, teacher collaboration, and ongoing professional development of faculty and staff. In addressing functional roles of persons in a professional group, they also point out another set of roles and behaviors, called dysfunctional, which distract a group from its task(s). Those employed to cultivate our greatest natural resource, our young, must set high expectations (Edmonds, 1979; Levine & Lezotte, 1990) for them and accept nothing less than their best. The belief that all children can learn, according to Edmonds, must be manifested in the teacher's behavior.

Education is often seen as a means of personal development. Plato viewed education as a process that elicits the knowledge with which people were born. Froebel believed that there are dormant seeds of knowledge within each child that can be awakened with time and space (McNergney & Herbert, 1995).

Whether we conclude that the central purpose of American education is to create a thinking individual, or we believe in effective schools research, or we believe education is tapping what is within or developing what people are born with, an effective plan for improving instruction in order to improve student achievement must be founded on what we, as educators, believe.

The focus should be on helping the internal stakeholders to be more aware of their own philosophical beliefs, and to understand how their own beliefs guide the instructional process. Research supports that certain philosophical beliefs are related to desirable student performance. Those beliefs must be identified, accepted, and incorporated into a school's philosophy of education in the quest of academic excellence.

SAMPLE SCHOOL PHILOSOPHY OF EDUCATION STATEMENT

A model of a school's philosophy of education statement is the one created by Chapnick (2009):

Teaching combines knowledge, skill, passion, and compassion. [We] believe:

1. Students are people. They are proud, confident, eager to learn, but also insecure. They respond to people who make them feel listened to and respected; people who challenge them and inspire them to question; people who reward their successes and encourage them to improve.

2. Teachers are role models both in the classroom and in the community. Students look up to teachers whom they respect, and good teachers take pride in learning from their students.
3. Preparation and enthusiasm are cornerstones of effective teaching. They are contagious and inspire success. Successful teachers are committed and dedicated to improving themselves and their students.
4. Good teachers always try to be fair. They do not ask from their students that which they would not ask from themselves. They communicate high, yet realistic and achievable expectations, and then encourage students to overachieve. They recognize that students learn in different ways and respond differently to a variety of forms of instruction and assessment. They develop lessons and evaluate student progress with the diversity of student learning styles and backgrounds in mind.
5. Students learn best when they are aware of not only what is required of them, but also what is fair to require from their teachers. Just as students must meet strict analytical and temporal expectations, teachers should mark thoroughly and return assignments promptly. Feedback should be detailed, and means of improvement should be outlined specifically. Students should be congratulated for their achievements, and shown how to learn from their mistakes.
6. Effective teaching requires flexibility. Teachers must try to make themselves available to meet with students and explore their concerns both inside and outside of the classroom. Students are more likely to require assistance when assignments are due, and teachers should endeavor as best they can to schedule academic and personal commitments accordingly.
7. Teaching can always be improved. Professional development—remaining abreast of pedagogical advancements in the field, taking advantage of changes in academic technology, promoting the importance of teaching in the community, and maintaining a research program which expands the depth and breadth of knowledge of the teaching subject matter—is crucial to an instructor's long term effectiveness. Academic colleagues, teaching assistants, and student evaluations are all invaluable sources of assistance. (p. 8)

The following is another sample of a school philosophy statement created for Beveridge School in Gary, Indiana.

> Beveridge Elementary School faculty and staff care about, love, and cherish our students. We believe if we show our students we care about them, we create a positive, supportive relationship that helps us build a climate where learning can flourish. We aim to be intentionally inviting with our students, modeling the behavior we want our students to learn and emulate. We want students to

know that we are approachable. We believe that teachers impart more by way of example than precept and that students are perceptive and know when teachers are genuine. We believe in the power of a loving touch, a warm smile, a sincere compliment, an encouraging word, a listening ear, and all other acts of caring. We will take the time to connect with our students, to get to know our students, and to address all of their needs. We care about the whole child and want all of our students to be successful. We believe that every effort we make to show we care will be manifested in greater student achievement.

We believe that each child is a unique individual who needs a secure and stimulating atmosphere in which to study, grow, and mature emotionally, intellectually, physically, and socially. With this in mind, we believe it is our responsibility to create an environment that is supervised and safe, orderly but not controlling. We aim to motivate and stimulate all of our students so that they, not only want to, but are eager to come to school. We want our students to be intrinsically motivated. We will treat our students like they are our own children, providing the best, treating them all fairly and giving them the highest level of respect. We want our students to be shining examples for students at other schools.

We believe that children learn, not for school, but for life. Therefore, we will do our utter best to lay a strong foundation so our students are college and career ready. We want our students to be critical thinkers so we will stimulate thinking and provide meaningful, relevant learning experiences. Students will be encouraged to think in rational ways, so that they can apply their knowledge and skills in real-life and unfamiliar situations. We will focus on thought patterns (trends and patterns), instead of emphasizing rote memorization of facts. We will infuse rigor, relevance, and relationship into our classroom instruction. We will make sure that students master the basics, but we will not stifle creativity; students will have freedom that allows for expression and creativity. In fact, we will celebrate creativity. We will challenge our students and watch them grow academically to their fullest potential.

We believe preparation and delivery are fundamental to effective teaching. As teachers, we will always arrive in the classroom prepared for the teacher act, aiming to giving a presentation worthy of an Academy Award. Instruction and the curriculum will be molded to address each student's learning style. We believe that the teacher's role is to guide, providing access to information rather than acting as the primary source of information. Therefore, we believe in discovery learning, hands-on activities, and group instruction. We believe in and will seek ways to motivate and capture the attention of our students. As teachers, we will be flexible and adapt instruction to the teachable moment. We will take time to evaluate and assess so that we meet their needs. We will work to better ourselves as instructors of young minds; so, we will seek and use best practices. We believe in professional development and will insist that all in servicing is meaningful, data driven, and directed at improving instruction to increase student learning.

We believe that we cannot successfully educate our students without the assistance of parents and the community. Parents and others are welcomed in this school. They will be a part of school planning and every effort will be made to keep parents and others informed of academic program and school activities. We encourage parents and community members to be active in the delivery of instructional services. Training will be offered so that their involvement is most productive. We will provide opportunities to empower parents so they can aid the school in ensuring that our students are ready for future challenges. We believe that together we can successfully, not school, but educate our students.

In closing this chapter, focus your attention on the words of Zmuda et al. (2004) who note that incompetency or competency of a school depends on how the system is understood by key stakeholders. In competent systems administrators and teachers discern what "can be" by bringing to the surface the school's underlying purpose and the stakeholders' deeply held beliefs. They add, "Once educators, through collegial conversations, see the school as a complex living system with purpose, they can then understand their work, both individual and collective, as contributing to the continuous improvement of the school" (p. 30).

A school's philosophy gives collective purpose to the system. Educational leaders must lead the articulation and consensus building of a school's philosophy and then must consistently remind key stakeholders of those deeply held, defining beliefs that give purpose to educators' work and lead the stakeholders toward a common purpose. "For a school to be more than a loose confederation of independent learning environments, all stakeholders must be clear on the beliefs that give collective and concrete purpose to their individual efforts" (p. 40). Unified, collective core beliefs become the foundation for a shared vision and enable a school improvement plan to become purposeful and systemic.

REFERENCES

Beswick, K. (2005). The beliefs/practice connection in broadly defined contexts. *Mathematics Education Research Journal, 17*(2), 39–68.

Bredo, E. (2002). How can philosophy of education be both viable and good? *Educational Theory, 52*(3) 263–271.

Center for Public Education (2006). *Q and A: Standardized tests and their impact on schooling.* Retrieved October 9, 2014, from http://www.nsba.org/site.view.asp

Chapnick, A. (2009). Teaching philosophy and assumptions. In Faculty Focus Special Report. Philosophy of teaching statements: Examples and tips on how to write a teaching philosophy statement. Retrieved October 10, 2014, from www.facultyfocus.com/wp-content/uploads/images/Philo-of-Teaching

Edmonds, R. (1979). Effective schools for the urban poor. *Educational Leadership, 37*(1), 15–24.

Glickman, C. D., Gordon, S. P., & Ross-Gordon, J. M. (2005). *The basic guide to supervision and instructional leadership.* Boston, MA: Pearson.

Glickman, C. D., Gordon, S. P., & Ross-Gordon, J. M. (2010). *Supervision and instructional leadership: A developmental approach.* Boston, MA: Pearson.

Glickman, C. D., & Tamashiro, R. T. (1980). Determining one's beliefs regarding teacher supervision. *Bulletin, 64*(440), 74–81.

Hummel, J. H., & Huitt, W. (1994, February). What you measure is what you get. *ASCD Reporter,* 10–11.

Kagan, D. M. (1992). Implications of research on teacher beliefs. *Educational Psychologist, 27*(1), 65–90.

Levine, D. V., & Lezotte, W. (1990). *Unusually effective schools: A review and analysis of research practices.* Madison, WI: National Center for Effective Schools Research and Development.

McNergney, R., & Herbert, J. M. (1995). *Foundations of education.* Boston, MA: Allyn and Bacon.

Nespor, J. (1987). The role of beliefs in the practice of teaching. *Journal of Curriculum Studies, 19*(4), 317–328.

Nolan, J., & Hoover, L. (2008). *Teacher supervision and evaluation: Theory into practice.* Hoboken, NJ: John Wiley & Sons, Inc.

Pajares, F. (1992). Teachers' beliefs and educational research: Cleaning up a messy construct. *Review of Educational Research, 62*(3), 307–332.

Palmer, P. J. (1998). *The courage to teach.* San Francisco, CA: Jossey-Bass.

Sergiovanni, T. J., & Starratt, R. J. (1983). *Supervision: Human perspectives* (3rd ed.). New York: McGraw-Hill.

Tas, S. (2011). Management philosophies of primary school principals. *Education, 131*(3), 565–579.

Trigwell, K., & Prosser, M. (1997). Towards an understanding of individual acts of teaching and learning. *Higher Education Research & Development, 16*(2), 241–252.

University of Minnesota. *Teaching Philosophy Template.* www1.umn.edu/ohr/prod/groups/ohr/@pub/@ohr/documents/asset/ohr. . .

Witcher, A., Sewall, A., Arnold, L., & Travers, P. (2001). Teaching, leading, learning: It's all about philosophy. *The Clearing House, 75*(5), 277–279.

Zmuda, A., Kuklis, R., & Kline, E. (2004). *Transforming schools: Creating a culture of continuous improvement.* Alexandria, VA: Association for Supervision and Curriculum Development.

Chapter 3

The Vision

Many people view our public schools as failing, weak, sick, and places of academic decay. Those of us who believe in public education cannot accept the cynic's views and buy into the cynicism. Our schools are not as bad as they are portrayed, but we cannot argue against the need for visionary leadership to make our schools better and create schools of excellence. We can improve our schools. We can become what we want to be. Even though our schools are not as bad as they are portrayed, we cannot be satisfied with the status quo. Seeing beyond our schools' current state and envisioning the ideal school will help to overcome the social decay that plagues our public schools. If we can dream it, we can achieve it. This calls for us as educational leaders to create, communicate, and shepherd our school's vision until it becomes reality.

WHAT IS VISION?

Sergiovanni and Starratt (2002) note that one's educational platform (addressed in chapter 1) is usually the unspoken foundation of a vision. What is vision? Deal and Peterson (2002) define vision as the ability to see something not actually visible. Vision is the image in one's mind of the ideal school (Ashby & Krug, 1998). It is an ideal picture of a future point in time. According to Clader (2006), "A vision points the way to a preferred future . . . [it describes] people and organizations not as they are, but as they desire to become " (pp. 81–82). Blanchard (2006) defines vision as "a statement that includes the purpose, picture of the future and values—it creates a deliberate, highly focused culture that drives the desired results of the organization" (p. 4).

Whitaker and Monte (1994) say a vision addresses the feeling and ideas of the whole staff and is the manifestation of its values, goals, and aims. Bennis and Nanus (1985) define vision as an uncommon ability to visualize a better future for an organization, a mental image of a possible and desirable future state for an organization. A vision statement becomes the mental picture of an optimal desired state of what a school wants to achieve over a period of time. It provides not only guidance but also inspiration to the school.

A vision is indeed the driving force to increase student achievement in schools. Bolman and Deal (1991) after reviewing a large body of research on leadership note, "Vision is the only characteristic of effective leadership that is universal" (p. 41). Baskan (2000) in his studies found a vision not only improves education but also helps rebuild the relationship between a school and its environment in a stronger fashion. He stresses that such a vision needs to be based on cooperation among all internal and external stakeholders. Vision is key to the quest for academic achievement and excellence.

WHY SCHOOL VISION

In the book *Transforming Schools: Creating a Culture of Continuous Improvement*, Zmuda, Kuklis, and Kline (2004) outline that the second step of continuous improvement must produce the shared vision of the school: "A coherent picture of how the system will function when the core beliefs are put into practice. It is only when the school has a shared vision that administrators and staff can determine the gaps between what is and what should be and proceed toward purposeful staff development that nurtures and advances a competent system" (p. 58).

Robbins and Alvy (2004) state, "While a personal leadership vision is essential for the leader, members of the staff are not involved in its development. Hence, a process is needed so that the staff can articulate a shared, core ideology and an 'envisioned future' for the school" (p. 8). They point to the notion that there are often multiple visions in an organization:

- *A vision of self as a leader* entails one's beliefs about the leadership role, how one should act, things one should and should not do, and one's code of ethics.
- *A personal leadership vision* represents one's dreams, aspirations, and hopes for the organization and its members. It is also based on a code of ethics and deeply rooted values and beliefs about what is important.
- *A shared vision focused on teaching, learning, and assessment* engages organizational members in forming a collective vision that everyone can buy into, because it is reflective of the shared values and beliefs that

place student learning at the center of all practices and actions within the schoolhouse.
- *A shared vision for the school community* embraces the notion that schools cannot operate effectively without an important partnership with the larger community. This partnership affords enriched, augmented resources for members of both school and community. (pp. 4–5)

They stress that "when these visions are out of alignment or not shared by all organizational members, individuals often perceive a lack of focus and the organization doesn't run smoothly" (p. 5). Hughes (1999) states that personal vision is crucial, but in a school setting it is the building together of the vision—the true dialogue among the parties—that gives life to the vision. Alston, Gorton, and Snowden (2006) state that "there is little doubt that the involvement and cooperation of many people will be necessary for the successful implementation of school improvement" (p. 122). This statement suggests that principals need to make sure the vision is a "shared vision." According to Glickman et al. (2014),

> It is important that the purpose of such discussions not be to merely create a traditional vision statement, but rather to engage in open, reflective, ongoing discussion about how the school community can improve student learning by improving instruction at both the school and classroom level. The collective vision that emerges from instructional dialogue should be flexible and subject to change if it does not lead to the improvement of teaching and learning. (p. 11)

They add, "In dynamic schools teachers do not view their work as simply what they carry out within their own four walls but see themselves as part of the larger enterprise of complementing and working with each other to educate students" (p. 35). It should be noted that in schools where teachers have not traditionally participated in school-wide instructional decisions, some teachers will not want to accept school-wide instructional responsibilities or want to be involved in the process of effective school planning. A school leader who is a real change agent will work to unfreeze old mind-sets and behaviors by creating the conditions for change—building trust, demonstrating openness, and practicing inclusion. He or she moves the internal stakeholders from seeing him or her as the sole provider of instructional leadership to the coordinator or facilitator of instructional improvement.

Glickman et al. (2014) stress that successful schools have internal stakeholders who have "'a cause beyond oneself.' ... A cause beyond oneself ... is a common cause based on shared beliefs and core values. We can refer to this common cause as the school's vision, but to do so accurately, we must understand what goes into its development" (p. 35).

Every school has room for improvement, and if a school wants to progress, it needs to establish a vision for all stakeholders. Effective school leaders develop and support visions that lead to improved instruction and better student performance. Educational leaders must understand the importance of their motivating and leading others to reach ambitious goals (Cuban, 1988). The effective school leader will imagine what the organization can become, define its mission, set the goals, establish objectives, and link the vision and mission to organizational routines and behaviors.

George and Sabhapathy (2010) note, "The transformational leader inspires and motivates followers to perform beyond their self interest and to work toward a kind of greater good by appealing to a self of higher ideals and moral values and through buying into clearly communicated visions and goals" (p. 2). A school must have a vision that all stakeholders identify as a common direction for the school—something that gives them a desire to achieve, something that drives them to improvements, something that will not let them be satisfied with the status quo. A vision statement is based on the beliefs, ideas, and inputs of building principals, teachers, students, parents, and community members.

LEADERSHIP ROLE IN VISIONING

Leadership is an important element in developing a school vision, according to Licata and Harper (2001). Although the vision of a school is created through the involvement of many, it is the primary responsibility of the education leader to develop and effectively communicate the vision to all stakeholders. Hargreaves (2003) asserts that principals use their managerial skills to produce budgets and agendas with plans and use their leadership skills to build vision, goals, and strategies to implement plans. Tirozzi (2001) believes that "the principal's role must shift from a focus on management and administration to a focus on leadership and vision on facilitating the teaching and learning process" (p. 439).

Sigford (2006) insists that both leadership and management skills are significant and interdependent since the leader creates a vision to guide the school and the key function of the manager is to put that vision into action. Regardless, the building principal, along with other school leaders, plays a major role in developing, achieving, and maintaining the school's vision. Capturing the vision of the school in a vision statement collaboratively not only provides a starting point for improvement, but it also helps to direct the management and instructional decisions made, which help to move the organization toward the vision. The vision that is effective in producing positive change is an outcome of a cooperative effort closely related to the leadership style of the principal and other school leaders.

Robbins and Alvy (2004) stress that when the vision is just embraced by the principal or the school leaders, and not by organizational members, individuals may go through the motions or respond to pressure rather than as a result of deep commitment. The vision, the picture of the future, must be so beautiful that it attracts, captivates, and stimulates followers. It must loose educators who are bound by traditions, hiding under the cloaks of unions, and otherwise nonintrinsically motivated to seek excellence. Whether or not this happens depends on the leadership of the principal and other school leaders.

Often building leaders operated in a school system with centralized administration that is tightly controlled, and thus the central administrators are part of the problem. In the first generation of effective school research, Edmonds (1979) advocated that change comes school by school, not classroom by classroom. In the second generation of school research Lezotte (1991) supported this but added that for change to be more effective it needs to have the support of the central office. According to Korkmaz (2006), "A school which faces an obstacle due to the structure of the system will not operate successfully, unless it has a shared feeling or a common vision. It is a fact that the existence of a shared vision increases the effectiveness of a school" (p. 18).

Korkmaz goes on to cite Licata and Harper (2001) noting a robust school vision might best be expressed by harmony within the school—harmony that grabs the attention of those inside and outside of the school and causes them to focus their attention on the common dream (Nanus, 1992). Those at all levels of a system respond to harmony among students, teachers, principals, and other school leaders. Commitment to the vision becomes visible when the leader inspires and motivates the followers to perform in unison moving beyond personal interest and to work for the greater good of students. Vision is tied to high expectations. Through a clearly stated and understood vision the educational leader ensures high expectations and can expect positive results for his or her school.

THE PROCESS

Stolp and Smith (1995) say, "To create a vision, the [school] members must listen to each other, feel empowered to change the [school], have confidence in their ability to improve their performance, think critically and gather data about where the [school] is at present, and hold strong convictions about the ideals that should guide their work in the future" (p. 61). The actual process stakeholders choose to take in creating a vision may vary; however, creating a vision entails sharing of ideas and beliefs, making a commitment to make decisions and take action aligned with the consensus of beliefs. The resulting vision statement should be succinctly so that all stakeholders may be able to state it at any given time. The following four-phased process chosen by Smith (2013) and used with graduate students could be used in developing and realizing a vision.

How are schools today? A precursory listing of views of schools given by practicing teachers in one of Smith's various administration classes includes, but is not limited to, these following evaluative comments:

- Underfunded
- Mere caretakers of students, too many of whom defy authority
- Widely unaccountable
- Staffed with teachers who feel overloaded, stressed, and who impart negative feeling
- Stressful
- Victims of lawsuits
- Lacking in community involvement
- Full of indifference
- Reflective of societal ills
- Inundated with more and more state guidelines
- Filled with aging staffs
- Overwhelmed by societal pressures on the curriculum

These items identified in the *observational phase* leads us to ask: Why are schools as they are? Practicing teachers in Smith's classes noted the following societal problems:

- The breakdown of family structure
- Lack of community support
- Increasing presence of community apathy
- Low student self-esteem
- Presence of more mature students
- Too much negative peer pressure
- Influenced by a drug, alcoholic culture
- Negative television influence
- Reactionary problem-solving
- Breakdown of values or value changes
- Low staff morale
- Teacher "burn-out"
- Pronounced disciplinary problems
- Lack of adequate funding
- Low student expectation

The Vision

Not becoming depressed by those conditions listed in the *analysis phase*, it is at this point the vision becomes primary, and we ask: How can schools be? According to surveyed practicing teachers, schools can be:

- Environments where children succeed
- Arenas where children reach their fullest potential
- Centers of community involvement and leadership
- Filled with teachers who assume more responsibility
- Models for society
- Caring and nurturing organizations
- Motivation agents
- Respected
- Student-centered
- Positive focal points of the community
- Places where dreams are stimulated; in some cases, fulfilled
- Havens of cooperative efforts and shared ownership

Recognizing that dreams detailed here in the *visionary phase* do not become reality under their own powers, we ask: What is needed? What are the keys to make the vision happen? The teacher responses during the *implementation phase* include:

- Increased resources
- Increased parental skills
- Increased communication
- Induced accountability
- Widely known, and accepted instructional goals and objectives
- Effective training and staff development programs
- Community incentive programs
- Sufficient staffing
- Shared vision
- Clear mission
- Instructional focus
- Understood and implemented action plans
- Ongoing staff development
- Formal evaluations of faculty, staff, and programs

While some of these items are not directly controlled by educational leaders, we should note that we cannot have an effective personnel management and development program unless we address those elements that we do control. This calls for an outline of goals and objectives that encompasses an outgrowth of the vision. It is unlikely that we will ever get there, if we don't know where we want to go.

While the author offers the aforementioned process for creating a vision for a school, there are several other approaches to developing a vision. Robbins and Alvy (2004) cite another approach that is to invite all stakeholders to come to consensus on the answers to the following questions:

- What kind of school do we want for our children and staff?
- What will students learn? How will they learn?
- How will students benefit from attendance at our school?
- How will their success be measured or demonstrated?
- Of all the educational innovations and research, which strategies should we seek to employ in our school?
- If parents had a choice, on what basis would they choose to send their children to our school? (Robbins & Alvy, 2004, p. 8)

After a robust discussion of the preceding questions, he suggests that a vision statement that encapsulates the stakeholders' responses would be drafted. Figure 3.1 provides a stakeholders participatory process for developing a vision statement that could involve all stakeholders.

It should be noted that there is another process that practitioners use in school to develop a vision. The principal drafts a vision statement based on his or her values and beliefs. The statement is shared with members of the school leadership, often the school improvement team (SIT) for their review and input. Once the SIT has had time to review, a revised statement would be created and agreed upon, if needed. Then the statement would be shared with the entire faculty for feedback. The feedback is reviewed by the principal, and SIT and revisions are made, if necessary. At this point, the shared vision statement would be shared with the staff for review and input. The school leaders again review feedback, and a revised statement is created, if needed. The process continues with parents, students, and community members until there is consensus on a final version. This final version becomes the driving force for school improvement.

School leaders will want to ensure that there is consensus among all stakeholders that the vision and mission statements together capture the spirit of what they believe and desire. Once the school leaders have agreed upon a vision, stakeholders should focus their attention on the mission of the school. There is a lot of confusion regarding the difference between a vision and a mission statement. Often we see vision statements that are actually mission statements and vice versa. While both are important and serve as road maps for school success, they have different roles in a strategic plan for school improvement. A mission statement converts broad dreams of your vision into more specific, action-oriented, and concise terms.

Materials Needed

- Chart paper
- Pens or pencils
- Large Post-it notes
- Sheets of paper

Steps

1. Lead a healthy discussion of what is a vision, sharing various definitions from academic literature.
2. Discuss why a school needs a vision that is captured in a vision statement.
3. Lead a discussion on how the school is viewed today with participants noting the strengths and weaknesses of the school.
4. Following the discussions, divide all participants into small groups depending on the total number of participants.
5. Ask each participant to reflect individually on how they would like their school to be at a future time. What would it be like? How will stakeholders feel? What will it be known for? Examples: a caring place; a haven of safety; a learning center; a place where all students master the standardized tests; a place where all students are disciplined; a place where all students value their education; a place where all participants pursue excellence; a place where parents are actively involved, and so on.
6. Ask all participants to write each thought on the Post-its.
7. Encourage participants to share their thoughts with group members and as they do to post them on a piece of chart paper.
8. Ask the group members to select the four best thoughts to be shared with the entire group.
9. Reconvene the entire group and ask each group to report their best thoughts, placing the Post-its with each of the thoughts on a common sheet(s) of chart paper.
10. Via a show of hands, have the entire group select the four favorite thoughts.
11. Share with the group samples of well-written vision statements.
12. Ask each group to use the favorite thoughts to create a composite picture of a future state for the school (a vision statement). The statement should be written on a sheet of paper for sharing purposes.
13. Request a group to work with a partner group to share their statements and synthesize their statements into one.
14. Continue pairing groups and continue the synthesizing process until the entire group agrees on one statement that represents the shared vision of all of the participants.
15. If parents and representative students have not been involved in above process, the steps can be repeated with them, and the products of their work can be merged with the faculty and staff's work.

Figure 3.1. Stakeholders Participatory Process

> **Examples of Effective Vision Statements**
>
> Merrillville High School fosters an environment whereby all students become productive citizens and lifelong learners.
>
> Williams Elementary School produces students who master all state standards and are prepared for secondary education.
>
> All students of Gary Enterprise Academy are successful learners, responsible citizens, and productive members of a global society.
>
> Highland Middle School produces students who score in the top 10% of the state middle school students and exhibit socially accepted behavior.
>
> **Examples of Effective Mission Statements**
>
> Merrillville High School will strive to develop student skills for independent learning, responsible citizenship, and productive employment.
>
> Williams Elementary School aims to prepare all students so that they are successful in mastering all of the state standards and thus will be prepared for their secondary education experience.
>
> The principals, faculty, and staff of Gary Enterprise Academy via a unified effort, using individualized instruction and character education, are committed to empowering students to become successful learners, responsible citizens, and productive members of a global society.
>
> Highland Middle School will provide all the opportunity and motivation to learn, achieve, and succeed in a physically and emotionally safe, inviting, and stimulating environment with the shared support of educators, parents, and the community.

Textbox 3.2. Examples of Effective Vision Statements and Mission Statements

Vision and mission statements are related, in that they, both, look at the big picture. However, mission statements are more concrete, and they are definitely more "action-oriented" than vision statements. Your vision statement should inspire people to dream; your mission statement should inspire them to action. Mission becomes the means to the end result, vision. Robbins and Alvy (2004) underscore that a mission serves as a galvanizing force for achieving the vision. Hirsh (1996) points out that a mission statement is a succinct, powerful statement on how a school will achieve its vision.

According to Hirsh, the mission answers, among others, the questions: What is our purpose? What do we care most about? What must we accomplish? A vision indicates where you want to go (broad, abstract), and the mission declares how you are going to get there (concrete and specific).

Goals, objectives, and strategies identify how the vision and mission will be achieved. All of this becomes what we have come to label as a school improvement plan or an action plan. A process similar to one used to develop the vision can be used to develop other portions of the plan.

Educational leaders must take the responsibility for communicating the vision and mission for the school and shepherding the vision (Lunenberg & Irby, 2006). Vision and mission statements are not only a constant reminder of what is important to your school's stakeholders, but let other individuals and organizations have a snapshot view of who you are and what you want to achieve. The statements speak loudly, saying your school is focused and bound to a common purpose. When vision and mission statements are easily visible, a school's external audience learns about their school without investigating. To communicate the school vision and mission statements, schools have placed them on signs at key places in the building; in newsletters; in school newspapers; on bumper stickers; on T-shirts; on school stationary; and on pencils, notebooks, ink pens, and other "give-aways."

Vision and mission statements are often included in the morning announcement, used on websites, and shared at school events. For the vision to become reality, school leaders must shepherd the vision and mission. Stakeholders must constantly be reminded of the vision and the mission of the school. Instructional time must be protected and wisely used. In counseling students, educators should remind students of "the dream." Goals, objectives, and strategies are consistently discussed in grade-level meetings, department meetings, faculty meetings, and at parent-teacher meetings.

Lunenberg and Irby (2006) remind us to beware of vision detractors (i.e., tradition, scorn, naysayers, complacency, weariness, and short-range thinking), all of which can cause us to lose focus and to fail to achieve the vision. Visions must not be found only in documents; they must be alive and visible to stakeholders and observers. Robbins and Alvy (2004) conclude, "If a vision is truly shared, it will be evident in both the climate (how a school 'feels') and the culture (how 'business' is transacted) of the school" (p. 9).

REFERENCES

Alston, J., Gorton R., & Snowden, P. (2006). Major concepts in administration and the social sciences (Part I) of *School leadership and administration: Important concepts, case studies and simulations*. Columbus, OH: Opern University Press/McGraw-Hill Co.

Ashby, D. E., & Krug, S.E. (1998). *Thinking through the principalship*. Larchmont, NY: Eye on Education.

Baskan, G. (2000). *Action and vision in higher education in the 20th Century: Number 22*.

Bennis, W., & Nanus, B. (1985). *Leaders: The strategies for taking charge*. New York: Harper and Row.

Blanchard, K. (2006). Elements of top performance leadership. *Excellence, 23*(12), 4.

Bolman, L., & Deal, T. (1991). *Reframing organizations: Artistry, choice and leadership*. San Francisco, CA: Jossey-Bass.

Clader, W.B. (2006). Educational leadership with a vision. *The Community College Enterprise, 12*(2), 81–89.

Cuban, L. (1988). *The managerial imperative and the practice of leadership in schools*. Albany, NY: State University of New York Press.

Deal, H., & Peterson, R. (2002). *Vision of the leader*. Upper Saddle River, NJ: Merrill Prentice Hall.

Edmonds, R. (1979). Effective schools for the urban poor. *Educational Leadership, 37*(1), 15–24.

George, L., & Sabhapathy, T. (2010). Work motivation of teachers: Relationship with transformational and transactional leadership behavior of college principals. *Academic Leadership: The Online Journal, 8*(2).

Glickman, C. D., Gordon, S. P., & Ross-Gordon, J. M. (2014). *Supervision and instructional leadership*. Boston, MA: Pearson.

Hargreaves, A. (2003, January). *From improvement to transformation*. Paper presented at the International Congress for School Effectiveness and Improvement, Sydney, Australia.

Hirsh, S. (1996, September). Seeing and creating the future. *School Team Innovator*. National Staff Development Council.

Hughes, L. (1999). *The principal as a leader*. Upper Saddle River, NJ: Prentice-Hall, Inc.

Korkmaz, M. (2006). The relationship organizational health and robust school vision in elementary schools. *Educational Research Quarterly, 30* (1), 14–36.

Lezotte, L. W. (1991). *Correlates of effective schools: The first and second generation*. Okemos, MI: Effective Schools Products, Ltd.

Licata, J. W. & Harper, G. W. (2001). Organizational health and robust school vision. *Educational Administration Quarterly, 37*(1) 25–26.

Lunenberg, F. C., & Irby, B. J. (2006). *The principalship: Vision to action*. Belmont, CA: Wadsworth.

Nanus, B. (1992). *Visionary leadership: Creating a compelling sense of direction for your organization*. San Francisco, CA: Jossey- Bass Publishers.

Robbins, P., & Alvy, H. B. (2004). *The new principal's fieldbook: Strategies for success*. Alexandria, VA: Association for Supervision and Curriculum Development.

Sergiovanni, T. J., & Starratt, R. J. (2002). *Supervision: A redefinition* (7th ed.). New York: McGraw-Hill.

Sigford, J. L. (2006). *The effective school leader's guide to management*. Washington, DC: Sage Publishing.

Smith, V. G. (2013). *A540: Elementary and secondary administration*. Gary, IN: Indiana University Northwest.

Stolp, S., & Smith, S. (1995) *Transforming school culture: Stories, symbols, values and the leader's role*. Washington, DC: Office of Educational Research and Improvement (ED).

Tirozzi, G. N. (2001). The artistry of leadership: The evolving role of the secondary school principal. *Phi Delta Kappan, 82*(6), 434–439.

Whitaker, K. S., & Monte, C. M. (1994). *The restructuring handbook: A guide to school revitalization.* Boston, MA: Allyn and Bacon.

Zmuda, A., Kuklis, R., & Kline, E. (2004). *Transforming schools: Creating a culture of continuous improvement.* Alexandria, VA: Association for Supervision and Curriculum Development.

Chapter 4

Climate and Culture

Although educators have written about and studied school climate for 100 years (Cohen, McCabe, Mitchelli, & Pickeral, 2009), during the past few decades, in an age of increased accountability, climate and culture have become important focal points for school leaders. A growing and compelling body of research has established the correlation of school climate and school culture to the academic performance of students. Studies show the impact of both on school achievement, school response to change and reform, and on student learning. Research further substantiates that a positive school climate and a positive, sustained school culture promote students' academic success and healthy development (Cohen, Pickeral, & McCloskey, 2009; Center for Social and Emotional Education, 2007).

While Cohen, McCabe, Mitchelli, & Pickeral (2009) note that "a growing number of state and district leaders are considering sound methods of measuring and, most important, improving school climate" (p. 207), this book illuminates school climate and school culture because it is firmly believed that in order for school leaders to create school's of excellence, they must build or have in place both a positive learning climate and a positive, sustained school culture. The school's climate and the school culture become the ground in which we plant the instructional seeds. If the ground is fertile, well irrigated, nontoxic, and full of nutrients, it will produce more yield, bigger and better fruit. If the ground is infertile, it will yield less of a crop. Likewise in schools with good instruction, the better the climate and culture, the greater the degree of student achievement.

WHAT IS SCHOOL CLIMATE?

While educators have recognized the importance of school climate for 100 years and since the 1950s have begun to systematically study school climate (Cohen et al., 2009), there is no universal definition of climate. Definitions of climate traditionally focus on conditions as perceived by students, teachers, or others in a school setting that influence student outcomes. A variety of terms are used to define climate, such as "atmosphere," "feelings," "tone," "setting," or "milieu" of the school (Freiberg, 1999; Tagiuri, 1968).

Loukas (2007) define climate as the feelings and attitudes that are elicited by a school's environment. Hoy, Tarter, and Kottkamp (1991) contend that school climate is the lasting characteristic of the environment of the school that is felt by members and impacts their choices. Forehand and Gilmer as early as 1964 define climate as "the set of characteristics that describe an organization and that (a) distinguish the organization from other organizations, (b) are relatively enduring over time, and (c) influence the behaviour of people in the organization" (p. 362). Cohen et al. (2009) suggest:

> School climate refers to the quality and character of school life. School climate is based on patterns of people's experiences of school life and reflects norms, goals, values, interpersonal relationships, teaching and learning practices, and organizational structures.... This climate includes norms, values, and expectations that support people feeling socially, emotionally, and physically safe.... Each person contributes to the operations of the school and the care of the physical environment. However, school climate is more than individual experience: It is a group phenomenon that is larger than any one person's experience. School climate, or the character of the school, refers to spheres of school life (e.g., safety, relationships, teaching and learning, the environment) and larger organizational patterns (e.g., from fragmented to cohesive or "shared" vision, healthy or unhealthy, conscious or unrecognized). (p. 182)

Dorsey (2000) views school climate as involving four key relationships: the relationship of a student to himself or herself; a student to his or her peers; a student to his or her parents and community; and a student to his or her *school* personnel, including teachers, administrators, and all staff. Welsh (2000), in defining school climate, also focuses on interrelationships, but he adds cognitions in his definition; he says school climate is "the unwritten beliefs, values, and attitudes that become the style of interaction between students, teachers, and administrators. School climate sets the parameters of acceptable behavior among all 2005 school actors, and it assigns individual and institutional responsibility for school safety" (p. 89). Homana, Barber, and Torney-Purta (2005) state school climate refers to the beliefs, impressions, and expectations held by stakeholders about their school as a learning environment, their associated behavior, and the symbols and institutions that represent the patterned expressions of the behavior.

While early climate studies (Anderson, 1982) had a tendency to focus on physical, observable characteristics of the school's physical plant and conditions of the school, during the more recent past research has recognized that there are multiple elements that make up school climate. Cohen et al. (2009) write:

> A complex range of internal and external factors color and shape individual and, most important, collective experiences of school life—consciously and in unrecognized ways that we all pay attention to, remember, and attribute meanings to school experience as a result of our own internal experiences (e.g., fears and hopes) as well as interpersonal experience with students, school personnel, and family members. For example, if the majority of students come from families that have a pronounce view of school (positive and/or negative), this will naturally color students' experiences of school. In an overlapping manner, the school does not exist in isolation. The nature of school life is naturally affected by the district and community (local, state, and national) that it operates within. A multitude of factors color significant group trends that in turn shape the quality and character of the school or school climate (Freiberg, 1999). Although there is not one list of factors that shape the quality and character of school life, virtually all researchers agree that there are four major areas that clearly shape school climate: safety, relationships, teaching and learning, and the (external) environment. Although some state departments of education equate school climate with safety, the character of school life is clearly a function of multiple dimensions. (p. 182)

Based on the research of Cohen (2006), Freiberg (1999), and Cohen et al. (2009), these four areas and "subdimensions" of these four spheres are summarized next:

- Safety
  - *Physical*—people in the school feel physically safe
  - *Social-emotional*—positive attitudes and responses to individual differences, respect for school rules, and resistance to bullying
- Teaching and Learning
  - *Quality of instruction*—high expectations for student achievement, student engagement and rigor, respect for learning styles, creative methodology, and reward systems
  - *Social, emotional, and ethical learning*—cross-discipline instruction, appreciation of varied "intelligences," and relevant learning
  - *Professional development*—relevant in-service that is data driven, based on academic needs, continuous and systematic and evaluated
  - *Leadership*—visioning, excellent communication, administrative accessibility, and evidence of support for and respect of staff

- Relationships
  - *Respect for diversity*—positive relationships between all combinations of stakeholders, use of cooperative learning, involvement of students in planning, and honing student social skills
  - *School community and collaboration*—two-way school and community involvement, good communication between the school and the community (especially with parents), and shared decision making and responsibility
  - *Morale and "connectedness"*—enthused and connected staff and student body, pride in the school and community, and team spirit
- Environmental-Structural
  - *Cleanliness*
  - *Aesthetic quality of the school*
  - *Curricular and extracurricular offerings*

Although it is difficult to provide a concise definition for school climate, researchers (Cohen et al., 2009; Loukas, 2007) agree that numerous components comprise school climate. Cohen, McCabe, Mitchelli, and Pickeral definition states that school climate refers to the quality and character of school life, and it is evident in the way the stakeholders feel about being in the school. In the final analysis, climate operates in two domains, the physical and emotional domains, with multiple elements.

Physical Domain of Climate

- Appearance of the school building and its classrooms
- State of repair of the school building
- Temperature in the school building
- Condition of the grounds
- Equipment and supplies in the school building
- Noise level

Emotional Domain of Climate

- Safety and security
- Level of respect between stakeholders
- Level of caring
- Level of warmth and friendliness
- Bonds between and among students, teachers, and staff
- Equitable and fair treatment of students by teachers and staff
- Sense of connectedness to the school
- Level of collegiality

- Level of involvement
- Level of trust
- Level of academic expectations for all stakeholders

THE IMPORTANCE OF CLIMATE

Adelman and Taylor (2005) and Greenberg et al. (2003) express the view that school improvement requires coordinated, sustained, and intentional efforts to create learning climates that promote students' social, emotional, ethical, and intellectual abilities. Students who feel safe, connected, and engaged in school are more likely to learn or master more; research strongly supports the correlation of climate to student success. "School climate may be one of the most essential ingredients of a successful instructional program. Without a climate that creates a harmonious and well-functioning school, a high degree of academic achievement is difficult, if not downright impossible to obtain" (Hoyle, English, & Steffy, 1985, p. 15).

Loukas (2007) notes that researchers propose that it is the subjective perception of the school's environment that influences individual outcomes. She adds that stakeholders do not necessarily experience the climate of the school the same way, but, because of the importance of individual perceptions, schools often assess how students feel about their school. Blum, McNeely, and Rinehart (2002) and Osterman (2000) make the point that safe, caring, participatory, and responsive school climate fosters greater attachment to school and provides the optimal foundation for social, emotional, and academic learning. Urban (1999) states, "Unless students experience a positive and supportive climate, some may never achieve the most minimum standards or realize their full potential" (p. 69).

In addition to impacting the academic achievement of students, Loukas argues that school climate impacts student behavior and emotions. He states:

> A great deal of research shows that student perceptions of school climate affect academic motivation and achievement. Increasingly, research is showing that perceptions of school climate also influence student behavioral and emotional problems. Behavioral problems are characterized by acting-out behaviors such as fighting, lying, and cheating. Unlike behavioral problems, which tend to be external and observable, emotional problems are more difficult to identify because of their internal nature, but include anxiety, sadness, loneliness, hopelessness, and worthlessness. (p. 2)

Suggests that school violence is a reflection of the school climate. He pinpoints attributes of schools that contribute to unsafe schools: schools that ignore misconduct; schools in which teachers and administrators have disagreement about or do not know the rules; and schools where students do not believe in the rules. Conversely, Stockard and Mayberry (1992) identify factors such as high expectations among school staff, students, and parents for student achievement, orderly school and classroom environments, high morale among school staff and students, positive treatment of students, active engagement of students, and positive social relationships among students that positively impact school climate.

Loukas (2007) says that understanding how students feel about their school is an important first step in decreasing the probability of negative student outcomes. She adds, "The quality of school climate impacts student feeling of connectedness to the school and, in turn, the level of connectedness is directly predictive of how students behave and feel. High-quality school climates cultivate a connection to the school and in this way protect youths from negative outcomes" (p. 2). Clearly a school climate that creates a safe and orderly environment will impact and reduce negative student behavior. LaRusso, Romer, and Selman (2008) state that a positive school climate is linked to lower levels of drug use as well as fewer self-reports of psychiatric problems among high school students.

In a study deJung and Duckworth (1986) found that a positive climate is correlated with decreased student absenteeism in middle school and high school. Lee, Cornell, Gregory, and Fan (2011) found that a positive climate is correlated with lower rates of student suspension in high school. In addition, research (Berkowitz & Bier, 2006) indicates that positive school climate is critical to effective risk prevention.

The Alliance for the Study of School Climate at California State University, in answering the question, "Why make the effort to improve your school's climate?" lists the following benefits:

- Higher student achievement
- Higher morale among students and teachers
- Facilitates more reflective practice
- Reduces student dropout
- Better relations with community
- Increased institutional pride

Why is climate in schools so important? Does it have an effect on students' development and behavior? Deci, Vallerand, Pelletier, and Ryan (1991) are persuaded that a high-quality climate has the capacity to satisfy students' basic psychological needs for safety, belonging, autonomy, and competence. According to Watson (2003), when these basic needs are fulfilled, students are more likely to become engaged in and committed to the school and therefore inclined to behave in accord with the school's expressed goals and values. Hawkins, Catalano, and Miller (1992) call this phenomenon "school bonding." Students become more thoughtful, reflective, and willing to accept the authority of others. They are more likely to exhibit concern for and respect for others and maintain higher standards of conduct, according to Osterman (2000) and Schaps, Battistich, and Solomon (2004). Students become more supportive of the vision, mission, and goals of the school, and as a result the community is benefited.

THE DESIRED CLIMATE

Safety and the level of discipline of a school are major concerns for parents. Recent antisocial behaviors such as shootings, mass student fights, bomb scares, and other acts of violence that have plagued schools have increased the concern for a safe and orderly school environment. To promote safety and combat violence many educators have relied on traditional law enforcement methods, quick fixes. Metal detectors have been placed at school entrances, security guards have been employed to patrol hallways and school grounds, security cameras have been installed in the hallways and other key points in the school building, doors have been locked, and unannounced locker searches have been conducted. Although sometimes effective, traditional law enforcement methods have not always been the answer and may have negative side effects. Yet, maintaining a safe, disciplined learning environment has been, and probably always will be, a major concern of educators and others.

In the effective school, Lezotte (1997) says there is an orderly, purposeful, businesslike atmosphere, that is free from the threat of physical harm. The school climate is not oppressive and is conducive to teaching and learning. Teachers and other adults accept responsibility for supervising students at all times and everywhere during school hours. There are a limited number of rules that are clearly stated that help students and staff to know what is expected of them and that guide interpersonal conduct. These rules are communicated to all stakeholders and enforced in a fair and equitable manner; favoritism is not displayed. Research confirms that schools that establish, communicate, and enforce a fair discipline system have fewer behavior problems (Kawachi & Berkmann, 2000; Sugai & Horner, 1999; Wang, Selman, Dishion, & Stormshak, 2010). Furthermore, according to Cloud (1997), codes of student conduct should set unambiguous and high expectations for student behavior and should also specify consequences of violations of the code clearly, in writing, providing specific procedures to be followed in the case of a violation.

While typically codes of conduct focus solely on student behavior, Hernandez and Seem (2004) suggest that schools adopt codes of conduct that address behavior for all internal members of the school. Thus, the code of conduct should apply to staff members as well as students. They say all adults need to be able to model the behavior they expect from students, and students need to see that respectful and courteous behavior is expected of the adults as well as them. In addition, emphasis tends to be placed on what is considered inappropriate behavior. They add that it is also essential to specify what appropriate behavior is and to provide examples thereof. Often school personnel assume that students and other members of the school know what acceptable behavior is. This may be an erroneous assumption, and students in particular may need to be taught appropriate ways to interact with one another, they conclude.

Schools that have wholesome climates have teachers and other adults who are "intentionally" inviting. Purkey and Novak (1996) in their book, *Inviting School Success*, identified four levels of teaching. They found that some teachers are (1) intentionally disinviting, (2) unintentionally disinviting, (3) unintentionally inviting, and (4) intentionally inviting. At the intentionally inviting level, staff demonstrate an effective command of helping skills, a broad knowledge base, and unconditional acceptance and regard for themselves and others. They consistently create messages and invitations enabling themselves and others to feel valued and worthwhile. These beneficial messages become the building blocks upon which to construct a healthy, well-functioning self-concept.

Many educators, without giving it much thought, are good-natured and pleasant and easily establish positive relationships. However, being intentionally inviting means to do something on purpose for reasons you can voice and defend. Stressing invitational learning, Purkey and Novak note the importance of a positive self-concept in regard to school success. Among several skills of the inviting teacher they listed reaching each student, listening with care, and being real with students. Purkey and Schmidt (1990) note the inviting process can be professionally practiced by counselors and other helpers, enabling students to feel valued and worthwhile.

Foremost among the attributes of a positive climate is a sense of caring. Noblit, Rogers, and McCadden (1995) asserted that caring is "a belief about how we should view and interact with others" (p. 680). Chaskin and Rauner (1995) state that "caring . . . involves the ways in which individuals and institutions protect young people and invest in their ongoing development" (p. 671). According to Rogers (1994) and Noblit (1993) caring is a value, not a means to an end. Caring in its right context, they say, creates possibilities for learning and development to occur for children. Chaskin and Rauner (1995) note that some researchers hypothesize that an intensive experience in caring for others may have a profound effect on young people.

Caring is expressed in words. Smith (1999) addresses the power of words as they are used in the school, underscores the importance of educators being mindful of the potency of words, and stresses the need for thoughtful use of words. He notes that words have the power to make or break people. In a longitudinal case study relating academic achievement, rather than academic than failure, to language Juliebo and Elliott (1984) followed a child from birth to approximately age eight. They record his early success with learning language and reading skill and then discuss his academic decline after being labeled a low achiever and a candidate for remedial classes. Given the label "remedial student" in grade two, this once-bright, enthusiastic child adopted the label and behaved as a slow learner would. His schoolwork continued to decline. A transfer to another school was the beginning of the child's academic salvation. His teacher, using words, began to rebuild his self-concept, rewarding him for improved work and encouraging his endeavors. The school year ended with the child having B's in all areas of language arts. By the end of grade four he was awarded a commendation as the "Most Improved Student" in front of the whole school. Juliebo and Elliott (1984) conclude the study noting that whether or not the child will continue to grow positively depends on whether he or she again will meet a teacher who will destroy an already-fragile self-concept.

In schools with positive climates, all of the adults are aware that negative statements, put-downs, have no place in schools. They select their words with wisdom, choose the positive over the negative, and eliminate disinviting language from their vocabulary and professional repertoire. Additionally, they guard the students' environment limiting the negative put-downs students share with each other.

Caring is also expressed in deeds and behavior. Teachers who are striving to be inviting must recognize that negative behavior on the part of adults is just as lethal as words can be. Our actions speak so loudly that often students can't hear our words. Caring teachers watch their actions and responses to students' actions. They monitor and reflect on their performance in the classroom and throughout the school setting. Note, however, that teachers who genuinely care about students do not limit their caring to the words they choose; their caring mushrooms into their deeds. Because they care, caring is manifested in their behavior.

Teachers may be heard saying they care about their students. They may be heard saying, "My students know I care." But, do they? They may express their caring in ways that the students don't understand. Some teachers say, "I don't have to be nice to my students for them to know I care." They think that being nice means never correcting a student or never pushing a student to excel. But caring teachers do both, because they care. Other teachers express fear in showing students they care. They fear that getting too close to students leads to inappropriate behavior. In response, Meyers (2009) says, "[Teachers] must maintain an awareness of interpersonal boundaries when creating supportive relationships with students. Effective, caring [teachers] balance their connection with students by setting limits as needed, by enforcing classroom policies in consistent and equitable ways, and by maintaining democratic and respectful authority in the . . . classroom" (p. 207).

Caring teachers want their students to succeed and are committed to helping them achieve their goals. Moreover, these teachers care about their students' happiness, well-being, and life beyond the classroom. There are many behaviors that convey to students that we care. Among them are coming to class prepared to teach, greeting students each day as they enter the room, asking students questions about their experiences, actively listening to students, using a warm, inviting tone of voice, explaining why you are punishing a student, engaging students during the lesson, reflecting on your personal experiences during your lessons, using humor in class, addressing students by name, improving your instruction by learning something new, expressing concern about things going on in a student's life, being available to provide additional instructional assistance, responding to a student's personal needs, attending special events in a student's life, and many others.

Caring increases teacher-student rapport, develops strong bonds to the school, creates positive peer relations, leads to greater student enjoyment of the class, improves student attendance and attention, and increases study time devoted to the class assignments. A caring teacher can transform the school experience especially for students who face enormous difficulties, such as dropping out or dysfunctional home lives (Cassidy & Bates, 2005). Teachers often don't realize how even the smallest caring gesture can have a huge impact on our students (Eaker-Rich & Galen, 1996).

While there is less written in the literature about the *physical environment* as it is related to school climate, it is an important domain. A growing body of research (Evans, 2006; Lackney, 2005) connects the quality of school facilities both to student outcomes including achievement, behavior, and attitude and to teacher attitude and behavior. They suggest that the physical environment of their school enhances and/or impedes teaching and learning. "A school building that is run-down, or with bathroom stalls covered in graffiti and furniture falling apart, sends a message to students about their worth and the value of their educational experience. At the same time, students who deface or disrespect their school property are communicating their own feelings for their school, adults, and their peers. Giving students responsibility to help maintain and restore their school environment is a powerful strategy for improving school climate" (p. 16).

In schools with high quality of school climate, the temperature in the building is well regulated. Buildings are neither too hot in the summer nor too cold in the winter. The school leaders ensure the facilities are clean and well maintained. Repairs are made as needed, and the building is not allowed to remain in a state of disrepair. Noise in the building is ambient, and there is a sense of order in the building. The landscaping is pleasing to the sight, and the lawn is always well manicured. School decorations are used and updated to enhance the learning environment.

Schools with positive climates are collegial schools. The school is characterized by strong collaborative learning communities, which improve teacher practice as well as student learning through dialogue and collaboration around engaging classroom instruction (Marzano, 2007). In other words, when students, in partnership with educators and parents, work to improve school climate, they promote essential learning skills (e.g., creativity and innovation skills, critical thinking and problem-solving skills, communication and collaborative skills) as well as life and career skills (e.g., flexibility and adaptability; initiative, social, and cross-cultural skills; productivity and accountability; leadership and responsibility) that provide the foundation for twenty-first-century learning, according to the report by Partnership for 21st Century Skills (2002).

In schools with positive school climates there is a sense of high expectations. The internal stakeholders believe and demonstrate that all students can obtain mastery of the school's essential curriculum. They also believe that they, the school leaders, faculty, and staff, have the capability to help all students obtain that mastery and are committed to developing students to their fullest capacity.

In these schools high expectation is not a term; it is a lifestyle. School leaders have high expectations for themselves. They model excellence. They report to school on time. They research best practices and share them with other stakeholders. They are visible in the school, and they monitor instruction consistently. They take leadership in analyzing data and developing plans to address academic weaknesses. They are engaged with their students. They give respect to all stakeholders and demand the same.

Faculty and staff have high expectations for themselves. They come to school prepared to teach, and they protect instructional time. In quest of academic excellence, they reflect on their lessons and teaching. They are willing to try new ideas and strategies. Their lesson objectives and the goals of each lesson are posted and shared with students. While they strive to get parents involved and accept responsibility, they don't blame parents for students' lack of homework completion, engagement, or behavior but instead take a leadership role in trying to get all affected to respond and achieve. They find ways to motivate and engage their students. They don't allow students to demonstrate disrespect, so they don't disrespect students. They recognize that they must first establish high behavior expectations prior to implementing high academic standards. They don't enter into power struggles with students, and they choose their battles wisely. They strive to be inviting, and they build engagement into their lesson plans. They know that they demonstrate their belief in their students (or lack of it) by their comments, attitudes, behaviors, tone of voice, gestures, facial expressions, and body language. Their overall behavior reflects that they believe "all students can learn."

Students are encouraged to believe in themselves and to believe that they can achieve—that they can do things that is harder than what they have done or think they can do. They are not permitted to say, "I can't do it." They are held accountable for arriving at school prepared to do their work and do it well. Students are motivated to participate in class discussions and activities. Listening skills are taught, and students are held accountable to listen. Students are encouraged to try new things and reflect on their work and behavior. In all, students are taught to hold themselves accountable for their success or lack of it.

Parents are held accountable and become team members in the school's quest for academic excellence. Their attendance at Parent Teacher Organization/Parent Teacher Association (PTO/PTA) meetings, progress report conferences, and parent workshops is monitored, and steps are taken to increase participation and involvement. Parents are not allowed to consistently bring students to school late or to be late picking up their children. Parents accept the responsibility of providing a quiet place for their children to do their homework, assisting (not doing) their children in the completion of homework, and then monitoring to make sure their children turn in the work. Parents understand that they must be in tune with the school and support school rules. They never encourage students to fight, unless the student has no other recourse.

ROLE OF THE PRINCIPAL

As noted earlier and illustrated in figure 4.1, a complex variety of factors and forces shape the climate and character of the school. However, it is clear that the principal is the single most important factor of force. The leadership behaviors of principals are critical. Bulach, Boothe, and Pickett (1998) and Sergiovanni and Starratt (1998) relate principal behaviors to school climate, noting that the climate of a school is shaped by the actions of the principal. The Wallace Foundation Report (2006) also presents compelling research support for the notion that after the classroom teacher, the building leader is the most important "force" that shapes student learning. From a wide range of educational and organizational development findings, it is well known that the leader of an organization sets the tone and provides explicit or implicit norms of behavior. The extent to which the principal recognizes this and is prepared to shape a positive learning climate will determine the level of academic achievement in a school.

In a school with a wholesome, positive school climate, school leaders know how to support teachers in their work, and such support is perceived and appreciated by teachers. In a school with a healthy school climate, teachers believe that they are influential in affecting what happens in the school. These teachers have a "sense of school community" (Cohen et al., 2009). Why is this important? The emotional state of teachers directly impacts the climate of the school. Happy persons make other people happy, and sad people make other people sad. As educators, we should focus on the words of Ginott (1972) in his book, *Teacher and Child: A Book for Parents and Teachers*, where he says:

> I have come to the frightening conclusion that I am the decisive element. It is my personal approach that creates the climate. It is my daily mood that makes the weather. I possess tremendous power to make life miserable or joyous. I can be a tool of torture or an instrument of inspiration, I can humiliate or humor, hurt or heal. In all situations, it is my response that decides whether a crisis is escalated or de-escalated, and a person is humanized or de-humanized. If we treat people as they are, we make them worse. If we treat people as they ought to be, we help them become what they are capable of becoming. (p. 15)

Strong instructional leaders establish policies and programs, create processes, and consistently maintain a deep commitment to developing and sustaining a caring and academically supportive environment. The commitment is demonstrated in their behavior as well. They are not easily deterred from their course. When problems arise, they are able to work from their inviting stance to adjust their practices and grow through the process. Invitational leaders show a consistent and constant appreciation of all stakeholders and others. They have a democratic style of leadership and work hard to build trust among others. In summation, leaders who are committed to invitational education build goodwill and connectedness. Loukas (2007) defines school connectedness as student perceptions of belonging and closeness with others at the school. School climates that cultivate a connection to the school protect youths from negative outcomes.

WHAT IS SCHOOL CULTURE?

The literature (Gruenert, 2008; Schoen & Treddie, 2008) reflects that there has been some confusion between the terms "school climate" and "school culture." Often the terms are used synonymously and interchangeably;

however, school culture has a different meaning. Tableman (2004) states that school culture refers to the beliefs and expectations that members of the school community share about how the school operates. The culture of a school is what it is known for. It is represented by the shared beliefs, accepted practices, traditions, nuances, and other perceived characteristics that set the tone for the school. Culture is revealed in observable behaviors, but it is based on elements that are obscure: attitudes, beliefs, ethics, principles, and values (see figure 4.1). She adds that these are so deeply embedded and ingrained in the school that they are unconscious and often taken for granted. Tableman (2004) notes that a school's culture has characteristics that exist in multiple layers:

- Artifacts and symbols: the way its buildings are decorated and maintained
- Values: the manner in which administrators, principals, and staff function and interact
- Assumptions: the beliefs that are taken for granted about human nature. (p. 2)

She says that a [school's] culture develops over time and is maintained by several elements:

- Common beliefs and values that key individuals communicate and enforce
- Heroes and heroines whose actions and accomplishments embody these values
- Rituals and ceremonies that reinforce these values
- Stories that reflect what the organization stands for. (p. 2)

Gruenert (2008) makes it spring water, crystal clear that a [school's] culture will determine a school's climate. He writes:

> Whenever a group of people spend a significant amount of time together, they develop a common set of expectations. These expectations evolve into unwritten rules to which group members conform in order to remain in good standing with their colleagues. Groups develop a common culture in order to pass on information to the next generation. That information, however, represents a set of beliefs that have been passed down by imperfect humans with personal preferences. In schools, new teachers arrive with their own ideas about how to do their jobs. Through their schooling, they will have been immersed in theories of best practices and cutting-edge methodologies. If the culture of their first job does not embrace these new ideas, they will soon learn that to fit in they will need to assimilate. Because new teachers want to fit in and to feel like experienced teachers, they are vulnerable to the school's culture and all the unwritten rules that have been passed on through the decades. (p. 57)

Figure 4.1. The Nature and Elements of School Culture.

"School culture is based on past experiences which provides a template for future action based on 'how we do things in this [school]' " (Tableman, 2004, p. 1). Gruenert (2008) asserts that school culture is about "the way we do things around here" and school climate is about "the way we feel around here." The climate reflects the current physical and emotional conditions of a school, whereas the culture reflects what a school is known for. Culture is an ongoing process; it is not created or changed overnight. It takes years of established school climates to create a school's culture.

It should also be noted that as we address culture, we understand that there are aspects of school culture that are *observable,* that is, behaviors and habits, and there are aspects of the school culture that are *obscure*, such as attitudes, beliefs, ethics, principles, and values (see figure 4.1). Whether observable or obscure, school culture is a major factor that can affect and influence school improvement and reform efforts (McMaster, 2013; Sailes, 2008; Schoen & Teddlie, 2008). Deal and Peterson (1999) are of the opinion that school reform efforts are likely to fail if they are not meaningfully linked to a school's culture. Gruenert (2008) is convinced that "culture always wins" (p. 57).

THE PRINCIPAL'S ROLE

"Climate is the main leverage point for any culture, which means that if school leaders want to shape a new culture, they should start with an assessment of the climate. If the culture is ineffective, there are probably climate issues that were missed before they became rooted in the culture" (Gruenert, 2008, p. 58). Gruenert says, "It is easier to change a school's climate or feeling than it is to change its culture or personality." The author is agreement agree, but he believe it can be done. A strong, effective leader who is visionary and committed is key. The following is recommended:

- First, the principal must understand the difference between a school's climate and its culture.
- The principal must perceive what is the desired climate, the ideal.
- The principal must know the elements of the physical domain of climate and work to perfect each.
- The principal must know the elements of the emotional domain of climate and work to perfect each.
- The principal must strive for and demand high expectations for self and all stakeholders.
- The principal must hold all stakeholders responsible in the creation of a school's culture—custodians, lunch matrons, crossing guards, parents, community members. Everyone! Everyone has to sense the need for and be committed to contributing to the fundamental foundation of what the school is, how it functions, how it sustains itself, and how it develops.

The principal and other school leaders must lead the charge. If they are successful in continuously improving the climate of the school and maintain those improvements year after year, stressing high expectations along the way, then the school will develop a culture in which all can be proud. With a positive, productive culture a school will be on its way to becoming a school of academic excellence.

REFERENCES

Adelman, H., & Taylor, L. (2005). *The school leader's guide to student learning supports: New directions for addressing barriers to learning.* Thousand Oaks, CA: Corwin.

Alliance for the Study of School Climate. (2014). *Why make the effort to improve your school's climate?* Los Angeles, CA: California State University.

Anderson, C. (1982). The search for school climate: A review of the research. *Review of Educational Research, 52*, 368–420.

Berkowitz, M. W., & Bier, M. C. (2006). *What works in character education: A report for policy makers and opinion leaders* (research report). Retrieved from http://www.characterandcitizenship.org/research/WWCEforpolicymakers.pdf

Blum, R. W., McNeely, C. A., & Rinehart, P. M. (2002). *Improving the odds: The untapped power of schools to improve the health of teens*. Minneapolis, MN: University of Minnesota, Center for Adolescent Health and Development.

Bulach, C., Boothe, D., & Pickett, W. (1998). "Should nots" for school principals: Teachers share their views. *ERS SPECTRUM: Journal of School Research and Information, 16*(1), 16–20.

Cassidy, W., & Bates, A. (2005). "Drop-outs" and "push-outs": Finding hope at a school that actualizes the ethic of care. *American Journal of Education, 112*(1), 66–102.

Center for Social and Emotional Education. (2007). *School climate research summary*. New York: Author. Retrieved from http://nscc.csee.net/effective/school_climate_research_summary.pdf

Chaskin, R. J., & Rauner, D. M. (1995). Youth and caring: An introduction. *Phi Delta Kappan, 76*(9), 667–674.

Cloud, R. (1997). *Solutions for youth violence for schools and communities: A resource guide*. Waco, TX: Health EDCO, a division of WRS Group.

Cohen, J. (2006). Social, emotional, ethical, and academic education: Creating a climate for learning, participation in democracy, and well-being. *Harvard Educational Review, 76*, 201–237.

Cohen, J., McCabe, L., Michelli, N. M., & Pickeral, T. (2009). School climate: Research, policy, practice, and teacher education. *Teachers College Record, 111*(1), 180–213.

Cohen, J., Pickeral, T., & McCloskey, M. (2009). The challenge of assessing school climate [Online content]. *Educational Leadership, 66*(4). Retrieved October 8, 2015, from http://www.ascd.org/publications/educational-leadership/dec08/vol66/num04/The-Challenge-of-Assessing-School-Climate.aspx

Deal, T. E., & Peterson, K. D. (1999). *Shaping school culture: The heart of leadership*. San Francisco, CA: Jossey-Bass.

Deci, E., Vallerand, R., Pelletier, L., & Ryan, R. (1991). Motivation and education: The self-determination perspective. *Educational Psychologist, 26*, 325–346.

deJung, J., & Duckworth, K. (1986). *High school teachers and their students' attendance: Final report*. Eugene: University of Oregon Center for Education Policy & Management, College of Education. (ERIC Document Reproduction Service No. ED 266 557).

Dorsey, J. (2000, February 8). *Institute to End School Violence*. (Online) In End School Violence. Retrieved May, 2014, from http://www.endschoolviolence.com/strategy/

Eaker-Rich, D., & Galen, J.V. (1996). *Caring in an unjust world*. Albany, NY: State University of New York Press.

Evans, G. W. (2006). Child development and the physical environment. *Annual Review of Psychology, 57*, 423–451.

Forehand, G., & Gilmer, B. (1964). Environmental variation in studies of organizational behavior. *Psychological Bulletin, 62*, 361–382.

Freiberg, H. J. (Ed.). (1999). *School climate: Measuring, improving and sustaining healthy learning environments*. Philadelphia, PA: Falmer Press.

Ginott, H. G. (1972). *Teacher and child. A book for parents and teachers.* New York: Macmillan.

Greenberg, M. T., Weissberg, R. P., O'Brien, M. U., Zins, J. E., Fredericks, L., Resnik, H. (2003). Enhancing school-based prevention and youth development through coordinated social, emotional, and academic learning. *American Psychologist, 58,* 466–474.

Gruenert, S. (2008). School culture, school climate: They are not the same thing. *Principal, 87,* 56–59.

Hawkins, J. D., Catalano, R. F., & Miller, J. Y. (1992). Risk and protective factors for alcohol and other drug problems in adolescence and early adulthood: Implications for substance abuse prevention. *Psychological Bulletin, 112*(1), 64–105.

Hernandez, T. J., & Seem, S. R. (2004). A safe school climate: A systemic approach and the school counselor. *Professional School Counseling, 7*(4), 256–262.

Homana, G., Barber, C., & Torney-Purta, J. (2005). *School citizenship education climate assessment.* Denver, CO: National Center for Learning and Citizenship, Education Commission of the States.

Hoy, W. K., Tarter, C. J., & Kottkamp, R. (1991). *Open schools/healthy schools.* London, England: Sage.

Hoyle, J., English, E, & Steffy, B. (1985). *Skills for successful leaders.* Arlington, VA: American Association of School Administrators.

Juliebo, M. F. & Elliott, J. (1984). *The child fits the label.* D.C.: ERIC Clearing house. (Bib ID: 5482563).

Kawachi, I., & Berkmann, L. (2000). Social cohesion, social capital and health. In L. Berkmann & I. Kawachi (Eds.), *Social epidemiology* (pp. 174–190). New York: Oxford University Press.

Lackney, J. A. (2005). "New approaches for school design." In F.W. English (Ed.), *The Sage handbook of educational administration* (pp. 506–37). Los Angeles, CA: Sage.

LaRusso, M., Romer, D., & Selman, R. (2008). Teachers as builders of respectful school climates: Implications for adolescent drug use norms and depressive symptoms in high school. *Journal of Youth & Adolescence, 37*(4), 386–398.

Lee, T., Cornell, D., Gregory, A., & Fan, X. (2011). High suspension schools and dropout rates for black and white students. *Education and Treatment of Children, 34*(2), 167–192.

Lezotte, L. W. (1997). *Learning for all.* Okemos, MI: Effective Schools Products, Ltd.

Loukas, A. (2007, Fall). What is school climate? *Leadership Compass, 5*(1), 1–3.

Marzano, R. J. (2007). *The art and science of teaching: A comprehensive framework for effective instruction.* Alexandria, VA: Association for Curriculum and Supervision Development.

McMaster, C. (2013). Building inclusion from the ground up: A review of whole school re- culturing programmes for sustaining inclusive change. *International Journal of Whole Scchooling, 9*(2), 1–24.

Meyers, S. A. (2009). Do your students care whether you care about them? *College Teaching, 57*(4), 205–210.

Noblit, G. W. (1993). Power and caring. *American Educational Research Journal, 30*, 23–38.

Noblit, G. W., Rogers, D. L., & McCadden, B. M. (1995). In the meantime: The possibilities of caring. *Phi Delta Kappan, 76*(9), 680–685.

Osterman, K. F. (2000). Students' need for belonging in the school community. *Review of Educational Research, 70*, 323–367.

Partnership for 21st Century Skills. (2002). *Learning for the 21st century: A report and mile guide for 21st century skills.* Retrieved from www.21stcenturyskillsmn.org

Purkey, W. W., & Novak, J. M. (1996). *Inviting school success: A self-concept approach to teaching, learning and democratic practice.* Belmont, CA: Wadsworth.

Purkey, W. W., & Schmidt, J. J. (1990). *Invitational learning for counseling and development.* Ann Arbor, MI: ERIC Counseling and Personnel Services Clearing House.

Rogers, D. (1994). Conceptions of caring in a fourth-grade classroom. In A. R. Prillaman, D. J. Eaker, & D. M. Dendrick (Eds.), *The tapestry of caring: Education as nurturance* (pp. 33–47) Norwood, NJ: Ablex.

Sailes, J. (2008). School culture audits: Making a difference in school improvement plans. *Improving Schools, 11*(1), 74–82.

Schaps, E., Battistich, V., & Solomon, D. (2004). *Community in school as key to student growth: Findings from the Child Development Project.* In J. Zins, R. Weissberg, M. Wang, & H. Walberg (Eds.), *Building academic success on social and emotional learning: What does the research say?* New York: Teachers College Press.

Schoen, L., & Teddlie, C. (2008). A new model of school culture: A response to a call for conceptual clarity. *School Effectiveness and School Improvement, 19*(2), 129–154.

Sergiovanni, T., & Starratt, R. (1998). *Supervision: A redefinition.* Boston, MA: McGraw-Hill.

Smith, V. G. (1999). A note on the effective language on the perception of racial groups by majority group members. *Challenge, 10*(1), 105–118.

Stockard, J., & Mayberry, M. (1992). *Effective educational environments.* Newbury Park, CA: Corwin.

Sugai, G., & Horner, R. H. (1999). Discipline and behavioural support: Practices, pitfalls and promises. *Effective School Practices, 17*(4), 10–22.

Tableman, B. (2004). Putting the pieces together. *Best Practices Briefs, 32*, 1–10.

Tagiuri, R. (1968). The concept of organizational climate. In R. Tagiuri & G. H. Litevin (Eds.), *Organizational climate: Explanation of a concept* (pp. 11–35). Boston, MA: Harvard University Press.

Urban, V. (1999). Eugene's story: A case for caring. *Educational Leadership, 56*(6), 69–70.

Wallace Foundation. (2006). *Annual report.* New York: Wallace Foundation.

Wang, M., Selman, R. L., Dishion, T. J., & Stormshak, E. A. (2010). A tobit regression analysis of the covariation between middle school students' perceived school climate and behavioral problems. *Journal of Research on Adolescence, 20*(2), 274–286.

Watson, M. (2003). *Learning to trust*. San Francisco, CA: Jossey-Bass.

Welsh, W. (2000). The effects of school climate on school disorder. *Annals of the American Academy of Political and Social Science, 567*, 88–107.

Chapter 5

Recruitment and Development of Staff

RECRUITMENT AND SELECTION

Followed by the quality of instructional leadership, there is enough evidence to conclude that teachers have the most effect on student outcomes. In order to improve the quality of education, teachers have to be skilled and able to teach all students. Barber and Mourshed (2007) in the McKinsey and Company Report, which looks at high-performing systems in wealthy countries, point to the Sanders and Rivers study, which showed that if two average eight-year-old students were given different teachers (one effective and the other of poor quality), their performance would differ by more than 50 percentile points in three years. Their report also shows evidence from the then Department for Education & Skills (UK) that students whose progress is below standard at age seven have reduced chances of success at eleven and fourteen and very limited (6%) chances of leaving school at sixteen with the minimum expected level of qualifications.

Sanders and Horn (1998) and Jordan, Mendro, and Weersinghe (1997) in their research studies conclude that it is clear that teacher effectiveness is the major factor influencing student achievement. They add, "As more and more states codify academic standards that all students are expected to meet, the question of responsibility becomes paramount. If students are responsible for attaining the standards, then teachers are responsible for teaching them. If students have differing abilities to learn, then somehow all must still be presented with the opportunity to learn" (p. 7).

Needless to say, teachers have a powerful, long-term impact on students' lives. The best should be selected by a school or district. With this point in mind and the national demand for greater student preparedness and achievement in public schools, the need to devote increased attention to the recruitment and selection of quality teachers has become more evident. Urban, suburban, and even rural schools and districts must understand the importance of marketing their school or district with fervor. Beteille, Kalogrides, and Loeb (2009) note that in addition to removing ineffective teachers and retaining effective ones, more effective principals hire more qualified teachers when vacancies arise. They suggest that the hiring may be driven by proactive recruitment efforts by such principals.

In his work Brewer (1993) presents some evidence to suggest that the greater the percentage of teachers appointed by principals with high academic goals, the higher the student test score gains. If involved in the selection process, those principals tend to select more highly qualified teachers. Strauss (2003) also finds evidence to suggest that principals can affect student achievement indirectly through the teacher hiring process. Barber and Mourshed (2007) in their studies note that high-performing school districts to improve student achievement do three things consistently well. Number one on the list is getting the right persons as teachers. They stress that the quality of an education system cannot exceed the quality of the teachers. All of this suggests the importance of recruitment and selection of teachers.

Drake and Roe (1994) assert that "perhaps the most effective way to make long-range improvement in organizations is to have a sound recruitment program" (p. 218). "Both internal recruitment and external recruitment have advantages and disadvantages to the school district" (Lunenburg & Ornstein, 2000, p. 529). For staff stabilization, a school corporation should consider opportunities for staff to advance their careers through promotion within the district or system.

Internal applicants are already familiar with the district, have a known performance record that can be examined, and may be less expensive to recruit than external candidates. Also internal recruitment improves morale and loyalty among employees (Lunenburg & Ornstein, 2000). Internal promotion tends to build staff morale (Lunenberg & Ornstein, 2000). On the other hand, some recruitment and selection from outside of a school district has worth. This eliminates inbreeding and allows fresh ideas and approaches to be infused into the system (Lunenberg & Ornstein, 2000).

In the quest for academic excellence, the recruitment and selection processes are most important. The absence of or the failure to adhere to a human resource planning process and a school corporation's mission in recruiting and selecting personnel can cause future problems (Drake & Roe, 1994). Drake and Roe add that concerted attention to selection is critical to reduce future problems. Proper recruitment and selection can lessen the stress of building leaders who must respond to instructional leadership demands, according to Lunenburg and Ornstein (2000). "One of the most important instructional decisions a principal or superintendent makes is hiring his teaching personnel" (Lunenburg & Ornstein, 2000, p. 529). While we can fine-tune and sharpen skills, it is difficult, if not impossible, to make over people.

Educational and social issues often are inextricably linked; as a result, schools can become the battleground for legal disputes that involve individual and group rights (Hessong & Weeks, 1991). Selection and promotion guidelines can help avoid legal disputes and avoid discrimination against minorities and protected groups of employees. Equity is a legal requirement (Richards, 1988). Affirmative action has played a role in creating job access (Kowalski, 2003) and gives people an opportunity to succeed or fail on their own merit. It doesn't mean special treatment for minorities and protected groups. What affirmative action does is give all individuals equal opportunity to show whether or not they can do the job.

In the selection process, equity of opportunity should be considered. Lingering forms of discrimination should not interfere with selecting those persons most qualified to lead us in the quest for academic excellence. Drake and Roe (1994) note that if in the past persons were discriminated against in hiring or promotion, steps should be taken to redress the past inequities. They add that through the normal processes of developing a personnel plan, districts can put into place a plan that includes recruitment, selection, placement, and professional development that will assure equal employment opportunities.

On the topic of external recruitment one should note, "Most school districts today no longer enjoy the luxury of having qualified applicants simply show up at their doors. Limited numbers of new teachers and intense competition among school districts for these applicants mean that districts now have to employ the same kinds of techniques used by private industry to develop and attract potential candidates. A strong, coordinated marketing and outreach campaign targeted to the pool of applicants a district is seeking can make the difference between success and failure in its recruiting efforts" (Project TRREE, 2006, p. 7). The report suggests, among others, the following checklist for developing a strong marketing and outreach campaign:

- Establish relationships with teacher education programs
- Project a positive and creative image
- Provide referral incentives
- Improve the hiring process (streamline, make convenient, and swift the process)
- Recruit teachers through alternative routes
- Reinstate retired teachers (pp. 8–9)

In addition, it is suggested that you start your hiring process early and make use of data-driven recruitment. Offering contracts early to the highest-potential candidates increases your chances of bringing in teachers with the greatest potential to advance student learning. The use of teacher performance data will enable the principal to build a diverse, high-quality pool of teachers who meet the school's staffing needs. District data should be maintained to reveal those institutions that have produced quality teachers, and those institutions of high learning should be on the top of the list to direct recruitment efforts.

Frequent information sessions at colleges and graduate schools, hosting social events for prospective candidates, and providing financial and other rewards to faculty who recommend prospective teachers who are actually hired are some ways to identify and recruit the best. The use of online advertising, expanding your recruitment base, casting the net as far as is possible and reasonable, and the creations of a mentoring system matching teachers in your building with quality potential hires are some other recommended ways that have proven to be productive.

An essential ingredient for getting the right people to become teachers is to provide good starting salaries and to compete with salaries that are inline with other graduate starting salaries (Barber & Mourshed, 2007). Barber and Mourshed conducted international research of twenty-five of the world's school systems including ten of the top performers. Their study indicates that all of the top-performing systems, except one, pay good starting salaries.

Barber and Mourshed add, "A good salary is not necessarily the main or only motivation for teaching" (p. 20). In fact, in their research, they say "salary is rarely stated as the one of the most important reason for becoming a teacher, even in the systems where compensation is good. However, surveys also show that unless school systems offer salaries which are inline with other graduate starting salaries, these same people do not enter teaching" (p. 20).

Timing is just as important aspect of a good recruitment and selection program. Good candidates are snatched up every moment. Most districts seeking teachers conduct their efforts during the months of April, May, and June. Districts and schools looking for the best, especially those in urban communities, should consider starting earlier. Not only should a school district start its recruitment early, but it should also consider that a school district that takes more than ten days to respond to an application is missing the mark.

The lack of organization and responsiveness will leave a district with the leftovers. Potential hires need to be nurtured. There should be persons identified who will make themselves available at every stage of the process to answer questions and maintain interest in the district. Doing so will make potentials feel they are valued and respected.

Prior to selection, interviewing candidates is a responsibility that must be shared between the human resources department and other school district employees, especially building principals. In most districts the central office staff manage the application and selection process; once strong candidates have been identified, principals should be brought into the process immediately. Drake and Roe (1994) suggest that a cooperative relationship be established. Building principals and significant others should be given a chance for input into the final selection process. Drake and Roe note the interdependency of positions within the school system in order to fulfill the mission of the school system.

Recruitment entails attracting potential applicants for anticipated vacancies. The objective of the selection process is to hire individuals who will be successful on the job. Recognizing that people are programs (they make them succeed; they cause them to fail), the two processes, recruitment and selection, could never be more crucial to personnel administration and management (Drake & Roe, 1994).

CLASSROOM OBSERVATIONS

Barber and Mourshed (2007) acclaim, "The quality of the outcomes for any school . . . is essentially the sum of the quality of the instruction that teachers deliver" (p. 26). They add, "Top-performing [schools] recognize that the only way to improve outcomes is to improve instruction" (p. 26). In addition to test analysis, to improve instruction the educational leader, who is responsible for improving instruction, must make classroom observations. An educational leader cannot improve what he or she doesn't measure.

Classroom visits combined with student-achievement monitoring efforts allow effective educational leaders to monitor outcomes and to identify areas of weakness that can be addressed through professional development, thus achieving uniformly high achievement. The more overt the monitoring, the greater the academic improvement! What is inspected is respected!

Outside experts or national specialists have assumed the responsibility of curriculum development (Dogan, 2012). According to Clandinin and Connelly (1992) this approach separates curriculum from instruction, since the active participation of teachers in curriculum planning is limited and teachers are regarded simply as curriculum implementers whose role is to adapt official curriculum to their classroom. They argue, however, for the interrelated nature of curriculum.

Hale (2008), McNeil (2006), and Ornstein and Hunkins (2009) insist that it is a fact that there have been some differences, inconsistencies, and gaps between the official, formal, written, planned, and intended curriculum and the taught, operational, and experienced curriculum (English, 1980; Hale & Dunlop, 2010; Weber, 2011). In order to assure that the *intended curriculum* become the *taught curriculum*, educational leaders at the building level must get into classrooms and make informal and formal

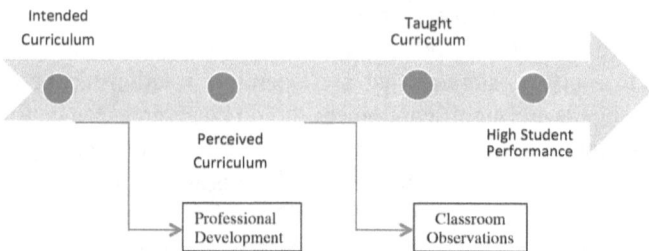

Figure 5.1. Phases of Curriculum

observations. Classroom observations allow the educational leader to determine teacher perceptions of the intended curriculum. In this age of the testing craze teachers seldom have a choice of selecting the content or goals of the instruction; therefore, they have to understand what official curriculum indicates. When the *perceived curriculum* is not inline with the intended curriculum, this calls for professional development so the taught curriculum can be inline with the intended curriculum. Without classroom observations needs would not be addressed. So in essence, there are three curriculums: the intended, the perceived curriculum, and the taught curriculum (see figure 5.1).

Additionally, classroom observations serve as an effective means of learning how certain teaching methods are employed in the schools, how classrooms are organized, and how students respond to the classroom environment. Classroom observation "[open] up a range of experiences and processes which can become part of the raw material of a teacher's professional growth" (Wajnryb, 1992, p. 1). Lunenberg and Irby (2006) note that "effective principals spend considerable time observing and coaching teachers in the classroom, which enables teachers to more effectively practice the art and science of teaching" (p. 203).

While there are multiple ways of observing, when teachers' instructional effectiveness is being formally evaluated in the classroom, most educational leaders use the clinical supervision model (Glickman et al., 2005). Goldhammer, Anderson, and Krajewski (1993) identified five major stages that principals can use in developing a reflective practice with teachers: a pre-observation conference with the teacher, the observation in the classroom, analysis and interpretation of the observation, a post-conference with the teacher, and a critique of the previous four steps, known as the post-conference analysis.

There are several performance indicator instruments. Performance indicator instruments allow one to record whether or not actions listed on the observation instrument have been observed (Glickman et al., 2005). A very popular instrument is Madeline Hunter's 7 Steps of Instruction, a lesson design well suited for direct instruction (Glickman et al., 2005).

Time management is critical in order for the educational leader to have time for classroom observations. Many principals spend a lot of their time "putting out fires," thus focusing the majority of the day to plant management. Needless to say, today's principals are busy. Lunenberg and Ornstein (2000) note that school administrators report that they do not have sufficient time to do everything that needs to be done. They have to not only be school managers but also be instructional leaders. Managing time is always critical for busy educational leaders. Proper time management is a strategy that can turn any school executive into a high achiever, according to Lunenburg and Ornstein (2000).

Walk-through observations have become a popular informal way to visit classrooms and are a powerful, efficient way for educational leaders to observe instructional strategies and interactions in classrooms or other learning environments. Although the process is simple, the data profile generated over time provides a wealth of information that schools can use to strengthen instruction and improve student achievement.

According to Lunenburg and Irby (2006), the walk-through method can assist principals in keeping in touch with the classroom and providing assistance to teachers in the quest for continuous improvement. Utilizing this method of observing, principals spend smaller amounts of time in a given classroom than they would if they were formally visiting a classroom; however, when combined, all walk-through observations can provide an overall picture of the functioning of instruction within the building, and can become a part of the evidence for areas of overall school improvement and correlated professional development, according to Fink and Resnik (2001).

In the quest for academic excellence, classroom observations are an integral part of supervision—improving instruction in order to increase student learning (Glickman et al., 2005). The assumption that one classroom visit a year is adequate does not lead to effective schools and increased student achievement. Time must be provided for educational leaders to get into classrooms, where the action is.

Barber and Mourshed (2007) state, "Most top-performing districts [or schools] recognize that no selection process is perfect, and so implement procedure to ensure that the lowest performing teachers can, if necessary, be removed from the classroom after appointment to their teaching position, based on the evidence of their classroom practice" (p. 20). It should be noted that the goal is to not get rid of lower-performing teachers but to identify instructional weaknesses and provide prescriptive professional development in order to improve instruction to increase student performance. Classroom observations are an imperative part of the process.

PROFESSIONAL DEVELOPMENT

Professional development, according to Fullan (1990), is any activity or process intended to improve skills, attitudes, understandings, or performance in present or future roles. Educators recognize that training is critical in helping schools to achieve the high standards set for them. Schools that achieve excellence promote and demand continuous professional development. Boyer (cited in Cunningham & Gresso, 1993) states, "The only way we've are going to get from where we are to where we want to be is through professional development" (p. 173). Professional development is the link to making sure the *intended curriculum* becomes the *perceived curriculum*, and once classroom observations are made, it becomes the link to make sure the *taught curriculum* becomes the *intended curriculum* (see figure 5.1).

"It is commonly stated that 'as goes the principal, so goes the school.' There is much truth to that statement, but even gifted principals can do only so much without teachers who know about teaching and care about teaching" (Sergiovanni & Starratt, 2007, p. 214). The ideal situation for all educational leaders would be one in which they could handpick and successfully attract any staff member desired, both certified and noncertified. Reality has taught us that seldom or never is this the case. Typically, educational leaders inherit staffs with varying abilities, motivational levels, stages of intelligence, and mind-sets. These variations combined with the restraints of union agreements, and tenure regulations make professional development quite challenging.

Occasionally we inherit a great faculty and staff, or through recruitment we are able to assemble an ideal educational team. Even in this case, one recognizes the need, with societal changes, to fine-tune and to grow. Needless to say, professional development must be a crucial part of any professional enhancement plan. Skilled as our staffs may be with change ever present, they need to go "back to the watering hole" or take time to "sharpen their axes."

Professional development should be an outgrowth of the school or district's desire to attain its goals and objectives. The process should begin with defining what superior instruction looks like. Barber and Mourshed (2007) assert that this task, which includes curriculum and its associated pedagogies, is challenging. The challenge, they say, is addressed by finding the best educators and giving them the space (and time) to debate and create a better curriculum and pedagogy.

The next task is assessing employee needs, including both instructional and noncertified staffs, and addressing those needs (Drake & Roe, 1994). Then the challenge is to develop and implement successful strategies to improve instruction (Barber & Mourshed, 2007). If educational leaders never get into classrooms to witness teachers in the teaching act and they never disaggregate data, they cannot know what needs their school's professional development program should address.

Strong, meaningful professional development programs are aligned with and driven by teacher instructional needs and test data. It is necessary for professional development to be prescriptive in order to be meaningful and productive. "Good professional development programs maximize employee contributions to the goals of the system and promote job satisfaction" (Drake & Roe, 1994, p. 225). Involving staff is slow and time-consuming but will prove most beneficial. As Drake and Roe note, effective programs may require the formulation of a district- or school-wide committee with broad representation of employee groups. They add that the professional development program is also the umbrella for in-service activities.

Of course, teacher can learn from each other. Teachers usually work alone; this denies them the opportunity to learn from and support other teachers. Educational leaders are encouraged to develop a growth environment where teachers are eager to observe each other's classroom practices, share knowledge on what works and what doesn't work, and shape a spirit of motivation and excellence that is contagious and cannot be confined. Remember that none of us as smart as all of us.

Sparks and Hirsh (1977) state that professional development should not be seen as a "frill" to be cut during difficult financial times. They say that professional development is an indispensable process without which school cannot hope to prepare young people for citizenship and productive employment. While professional development should be directed toward teachers as the primary recipients, it should also address continuous improvement for everyone who affects student learning, according to Sparks and Hirsh. Barber and Moursed (2007) write the following:

> Top performing systems [or schools] are relentless in their focus on improving the quality of instruction in their classrooms. Yet this focus on instruction, though a necessary condition, is in itself insufficient to bring about improvement. In order to improve instruction, school systems [schools] needed to find ways to change fundamentally what happens in the classrooms. At the level of individual teachers, this implies getting three things to happen:
>
> - Individual teachers need to become aware of specific weaknesses in their own practice. In most cases, this not only involves building an awareness of what they do but the mindset underlying it.
> - Individual teachers need to gain understanding of specific best practices. In general, this can only be achieved through the demonstration of such practices in an authentic setting.
> - Individual teachers need to be motivated to make the necessary improvements. In general, this requires a deeper change in motivations that cannot be achieved through changing material incentives. Such changes come about when teachers have high expectations, a shared sense of purpose, and above all, a collective belief in their common ability to make a difference to the education of the children they serve. (p. 27)

They quote a Boston policy maker who quipped, "The three pillars of . . . reform [are] professional development, professional development, and professional development. We align everything—resources, organization, people—with professional development" (pp. 26–27). This shared quote underscores the importance of professional development in the quest of academic excellence. Educational leaders are encouraged during the professional development process to keep Tim Duncan's quote in mind—"Good, better, best. Never let it rest. Until your good is better and your better is best (Duncan, 2015)."

REFERENCES

Barber, M., & Mourshed, M. (2007). *How the world's best-performing school systems come out on top*. Chicago: McKinsey & Company.

Beteille, T., Kalogrides, D., & Loeb, S. (2009). *Working Paper 37: Managing the recruitment, development, and retention of high-quality teachers*. Washington, DC: National Center for Analysis of Longitudinal Data in Education Research.

Brewer, Dominic. (1993). Principals and student outcomes: Evidence from U.S. high schools. *Economics of Education Review, 12*(4), 281–292.

Clandinin, D. J., & Connelly, F. M. (1992). *Teacher as curriculum maker*. In P. W. Jackson (Ed.), *Handbook of research on curriculum* (pp. 363–401). New York: Macmillan.

Cunningham, W. G., & Gresso, D. W. (1993). *Cultural leadership: The culture of excellence in education*. Upper Saddle River, NJ: Pearson Hall.

Dogan, S. (2012). *The views of teachers about curriculum mapping process* (Unpublished master thesis). Yıldız Technical University, Istanbul.

Drake, T. L., & Roe, W. H. (1994). *School business management: Supporting instructional effectiveness*. Boston, MA: Allyn and Bacon.

Duncan, T. *Good, better, best. Until your good is better and your better is best*. Quote retrieved on October 12, 2015, from Web site: https://www.goodreads.com/.../93387-good-better-best-never-let-it-rest-until-your-go.

English, F. W. (1980). Curriculum mapping. *Educational Leadership, 37*(7), 558–559.

Fink, E., & Resnick, L. (2001). Developing principals as instructional leaders. *Phi Delta Kappan, 82*(1), 598–606.

Fullan, M. G. (1990). Staff development, innovation and institutional development. In B. Joyce (Ed.) *Changing the school culture through staff development. Yearbook of ASCD*. (pp. 3–25). Alexandria, VA: ASCD.

Goldhammer, R., Anderson, R.H. & Krajewski, R. J. (1993). *Clinical supervision: Special methods for the supervision of teachers* (3rd Ed.). N.Y.: Stout, Rinehart and Winston Inc.

Hale, J. A. (2008). *A guide to curriculum mapping: Planning, implementing, and sustaining the process*. Thousand Oaks, CA: Corwin Press.

Hale, J. A., & Dunlop, R. F. (2010). *An educational leader's guide to curriculum mapping: Creating and sustaining collaborative cultures.* California: Corwin Press.

Hessong, R. P., & Weeks, T. H. (1991). *Introduction to the foundations of education.* New York: Macmillan Publishing Co.

Jordan, H. R., Mendro, R. L., & Weersinghe, D. (1997). *Teacher effects on longitudinal student achievement: A preliminary report on research on teacher effectiveness.* Paper presented at the National Evaluation Institute, Indianapolis, IN.

Kowalski, T. J. (2003). *Contemporary school administration: An introduction.* Boston, MA: Allyn and Bacon.

Lunenberg, F. C., & Irby, B. J. (2006). *The principalship: Vision to action.* Belmont, CA: Wadsworth Publishing Co.

Lunenburg, F. C., & Ornstein, A.C. (2000). *Educational administration: Concepts and practices* (3rd ed.). Belmont, CA: Wadsworth/Thomson Learning.

McNeil, J. (2006). *Contemporary curriculum in thought and action* (6th ed.). San Francisco, CA: Wiley Jossey-Bass Education.

Ornstein, A. C., & Hunkins, F. P. (2009). *Curriculum: Foundations, principles, and issues* (4th ed.). New York, NY: Pearson Education.

Project TRREE. (2006). *Annual Report.* ERIC Number: ED496528. http://files.eric.ed.gov/fulltext/ED496528.pdf

Richards, C. (1988). *The search for equity in educational administration.* In N. Boyan (Ed.), *Handbook of research on educational administration* (pp. 159–168). New York: Longman.

Sanders, W. L., & Horn, S. P. (1998) Research findings from the Tennessee Value-Added Assessment System (TVAAS) Database: Implications for educational evaluational and research. *Journal of Personnel Evaluation in Education, 12*(3), 247–256.

Seriovanni, T. J., & starratt, R. J. (2007). *Supervision: A redefinition.* New York, NY: McGraw-Hill.

Sparks, D., & Hirsh, S. (1997). *A new vision for staff development.* Alexandria, VA: Association for Supervision and Curriculum Development.

Strauss, R. P. (2003). The preparation and selection of public school adminstrators in Pennsylvania: Supply and demand and the effects on student achievement. Paper presented at the annual meeting of the American Education Finance Association, Orlando, Florida. Website: http://www.andrew.cmu.edu/user/rs9f/aefa_2003.pdf.

Wajnryb, R. (1992). *Classroom observation tasks.* Cambridge: Cambridge University Press.

Weber, S. (2011). The power of the taught curriculum. Retrieved November 5, 2015, from http://edge.ascd.org/_The-Power-of-the-Taught-Curriculum/blog/3326074/127586.html

Chapter 6

Rigor and High Expectations

WHY THE NEED FOR RIGOR

One doesn't have to spend a lifetime in education to understand that the field of education is filled with educational jargon. Rigor is the new catchword, buzzword in education today. It seems like everyone from all corners of our nation is either demanding rigor, in quest of rigor in the classroom, or deploring the lack of rigor in American schools. Colvin and Jacobs (2010) note that American public education has struggled with ideals of academic excellence and universal access since Horace Mann and the "common school" movement in the early nineteenth century. Generations of educators and politicians, they add, have stressed high standards with the valiant goal of helping all students achieve. However, events in the twentieth century have done more to usher in this term, "rigor."

Sputnik I did not only embarrass America but also generated fear. The nation responded to the security threat that resulted in education reform—a reaction that has been repeated since the 9/11 terrorist attacks. The early space success of the Russians not only challenged our nation's sense of superiority but also caused reactionaries to focus on our schools.

Education that had been left to educators for decades became more of a concern to noneducators. The crusade for reform grew more intense in the late 1980s. The Nation at Risk Report and a number of other reports raised numerous concerns about the low standards for students in American schools and concluded that our students are not prepared for the challenges of college and careers (Daggett, 2008/2014). Colvin and Jacobs point to the fact that it was in the 1980s that states began increasing their graduation requirements after warnings of a "rising tide of mediocrity" in America's schools. Blackburn and Williamson (2009) emphasize that since the release of a Nation at

Risk Report the debate about the quality of America's schools has grown exponentially; the call to increase rigor increases daily. They add that the adoption of No Child Left Behind (NCLB) intensified the debate raising it to a new level.

While the literature is mixed regarding the effects of NCLB on student achievement (Carnoy & Loeb, 2002; Dee & Jacob, 2011; Hanushek & Raymond, 2004, 2005; Lee & Reeves, 2012; Wei, 2012; Wong, Cook, & Steiner, 2011), most educators would agree that since NCLB in 2001, the era of accountability has placed an even greater emphasis on the need to heighten rigor in our schools. More recently the Common Core State Standards pinpointed the need for schools being held accountable for educating every student. Educators and our political leaders are increasingly focusing on the topic of rigor (Blackburn, 2013), and often these standards have been seen as the solution to increasing rigor in the classroom. Rigor in schools is touted as one powerful weapon to fight mediocrity and the threat to our nation's position in the world (Colvin & Jacobs, 2010).

So the pressure is on. Daggett (2008/2014) asserts, "Every district, school, superintendent, principal and teacher in this country is feeling pressure to get all students to minimum proficiency levels" (p. 1). Initially the accountability focus was on the educational leader, the principal. If school scores were too low, the answer was to replace the principal. However, accountability has now spread to the teacher. More states are demanding teachers to be formally evaluated. Education policies across the states are connecting student performance on high-stake assessments to teacher evaluation and retention. It should be noted that a key indicator of teacher effectiveness is the evidence of rigor in classroom instruction. It is evident that in response to weak U.S. student performance on tests, low college completion rates compared to other nations, the digital revolution, and increasing economic completion, political and business leaders are turning up the pressure on schools. So, is all the above the answer to the question, why rigor?

Jackson (2011) asserts that rigor is what makes learning robust, engaging, and appropriately challenging. Rigorous lessons by design go beyond a surface understanding of the material and foster students' ability to think and learn for themselves. She lists the following reasons why rigorous instruction is a valuable pursuit:

Rigor fosters persistence. When students must dig for the answers, they discover the value of the search. A little effort leads to small rewards, and more effort over an extended period leads to greater ones.

Rigor fosters resilience. When students learn to engage in rigorous thinking and inquiry, they learn how to manage and work through frustration to solve problems on their own. They develop a tolerance for uncertainty, acquire the skills and the disposition to handle struggle, and build a track record of overcoming tough challenges.

Rigor fosters flexibility. Rigorous instruction helps students grasp that learning is messy and unpredictable, and that understanding is something to be pursued through multiple pathways that are often complex, layered, and ambiguous.

Rigor fosters purposefulness. Students come to see that they are learning in order to make meaning, to broaden their own understanding, and to solve interesting problems.

Rigor fosters metacognition. Rigorous instruction asks students to think about their learning goals, select appropriate strategies for pursuing those goals, and reflect on the effectiveness of their chosen approach.

Rigor fosters ownership. When students must make meaning for themselves, they come to own what they have learned. Rather than be passive recipients of knowledge, students actively participate in constructing knowledge, filling in unstated information and imposing order on what they are learning. (Jackson, 2011, p. 16)

"More recently there is a growing recognition of the need to prepare students for life following high school—whether some type of higher education or employment" (Blackburn & Williamson, 2009, p. 1). If we believe that it is for life, not for school that we educate our young, we will do better. If we want the best for our young, we will do better. If we want our future young adults to be problem solvers and critical thinkers, we will do better. If we want our young prepared for an unknown future, we will do better. Wagner (2008b) conducted a study of American classrooms and concluded that even in some of the nation's "best" schools, students were inadequately challenged and were not expected to or competent to use critical thinking and problem-solving skills. If we take into consideration the needs of our students, we will do better.

According to Noblit (1993) and Rogers (1994) caring is a value, not a means to an end. Caring in its right context, they say, creates possibilities for learning and development to occur for children. So in answering the question, why rigor, the truth of the matter is that if we recognize the need and we care, we not only can but will also do a better job of providing instruction in an effort to improve student performance. Rigor in instruction is not the answer, but it is key. Furthermore, key to its presence in the school's instructional program, in its true sense, is the educational leader.

WHAT IS RIGOR?

While not scientific, to ascertain the level of understanding of what is rigor among teachers, several educational blogs were consulted. Shults (2007) in a blog, *An American Teacher*, notes, "There's a lot of talk in education circles today about rigor. Educators all over America are frantically waving copies of Thomas Friedman's, *The World is Flat*, as they attempt to awaken their colleagues to the impending doom our nation faces if we do not deliver a rigorous and relevant education to every American child. Politicians talk about the need to return rigor to the classroom. Parents demand rigorous programs for their children. School administrators performing classroom walk-throughs look for signs of it, and teachers are resolutely attempting to prove their lessons are full of the stuff." The previous quote was made in 2007, but years later in another blog, *Classroom Questions Q&A with Larry Ferlazzo*, by Education Week Teacher, Ferlazzo (2012) admits that he does not know what is rigor in instruction.

In 2013, in *Summing Up*, a newsletter published by the National Council of Teachers of Math, Gojak, the council's president, wrote, "Recently, I had a conversation with a group of math coaches who are working with elementary teachers on implementation of the Common Core Standards for Mathematics. The discussion turned to a description of rigor in the classroom. The coaches commented that many of their teachers were confused by exactly what was meant by teaching and learning with rigor. The coaches weren't sure how to respond." Williamson and Blackburn (2011) assert, "Few people question the need for America's schools and classrooms to be more rigorous. But there is little agreement about what rigor is and what it looks like" (p. 1). Certainly rigor is in vogue and will be the focus of the education agenda for the foreseeable future (Colvin & Jacobs, 2010), but many of those in quest of it not only don't know how to infuse it into instruction but also don't seem to know what it is.

In an effort to define rigor, let's address what it is not. It is not increasing the amount of homework, giving more worksheets to students who finish assignment early, requiring something extra on top of everything else, using higher grade-level textbooks for high-performing students, increasing the amount of reading, adding more assignments, and covering more material in shorter period of time, nor is it just for a select group of students.

Some states have responded to the need to infuse rigor into the curriculum by requiring students to take algebra, geometry, and laboratory science in order to graduate. Colvin and Jacobs (2010) note that five states in 2009 explicitly required that those classes had to be rigorous without defining the term. Since 2011, 45 states have raised their standards for student proficiency in reading and math, with the greatest gains occurring between 2013 and 2015, according to report published by Peterson, Barrows and Gift (2016). Incorporating more courses into the curriculum and demanding that they be rigorous won't guarantee an increase in rigorous learning in our classrooms. To sum it up: the problem is that people don't know what rigor means.

Williamson and Blackburn (2011) cite four myths about rigor in the classroom that are summarized here:

Myth #1: Lots of homework is a sign of rigor. Giving more homework is not rigor. All homework is not of equal use. Often homework is busy work and seen as unimportant by students. Often homework is built on the misconception that doing more of something must mean more learning (Vatterrott, 2009).

Myth#2: Rigor means doing more. Rigor is not defined by the number of assignments. It is not measured by the amount of things students must do, especially if the things are low-level and rote activities (Wagner, 2008a).

Myth#3: Rigor is not for everyone. Some believe that some students are less capable and thus we should lower standards and lessen rigor. Rigor, however, is anchored in the belief that all students can achieve given adequate time and appropriate and relevant support (Wagner, 2008b).

Myth#4: Providing support means lessening rigor. Some believe that assisting and supporting students lessens rigor; students must do things on their own for there is rigor. However, central to moving students toward more challenging work is the scaffolding provided to support them as they learn (Blackburn, 2008).

Blackburn (2014) lists three additional myths about rigor as summarized here:

Myth#5: Resources equal rigor. It is believed that buying new programs or technology will build rigor. The right resources can certainly help increase the rigor in your classroom. However, raising the level of rigor for your students is not dependent on the resources you have. Rigor is determined by how you use resources.

Myth#6: Standards alone take care of rigor. Regardless of how rigorous, standards alone do not assure rigor in instruction. Rigor is more associated with how you implement standards.

Myth# 7. Rigor is just one more thing to do. Rigor is not just another thing to add to your litany of things teachers are required to do to be considered effective. Rigor is increasing the level of expectation of students for what you are already doing.

Although similar, yet different, Jackson (2011) in her book, *How to Plan Rigorous Instruction*, also identifies seven myths about rigor that are presented here with a few slight modifications:

Myth #1: Rigor means more work. Rigor is about the quality of the work students are asked to do, not the quantity. More assignments or more reading does not guarantee a greater degree of rigor. In fact, rigorous classrooms often have fewer assignments and less homework.

Myth #2: Rigor means the work is harder. The definition of "rigor" leads one to think of strictness, severity, and difficulty, so perception of educational rigor being harder is understandable. Rigorous classrooms do present more challenges to students, but challenging doesn't mean difficult. Challenging work seeks to have students stretch their minds and acquire new understanding. On the other hand, "difficult" work can be difficult among other reasons because of unclear instructions, insufficient resources and support, and requirements that are too great for the allocated time.

Myth#3: If you have rigorous standards, you automatically have a rigorous course. Rigorous standards are aligned with higher expectations. How you require students to reach those standards is more aligned with rigor.

Myth#4: Rigor is a matter of content. Selecting highly rigorous content does not guarantee a highly rigorous learning experience for students. *How* one ask students to engage in the content determines the level of rigor in your classroom.

Myth #5: Younger students cannot engage in rigorous learning. Young children can be taught to think critically and process material in highly rigorous ways. Left to their own devices, children naturally have unique ways of solving unpredictable problems and dealing with uncertainty.

Myth #6: Rigor is only possible after students have mastered the basics. Any level of learning can be rigorous if you design the experience to be so. For example, students learning even the most basic material can be asked to build representations, organize facts, analyze and construct relationships among facts, and make inferences beyond what is explicitly presented in class.

Myth#7: Rigor is for the elite. Reserving rigorous learning opportunities for an elite group of students while relegating other students to rote learning and less meaningful activities is unethical; it leaves the majority of students unprepared to meet the demands of the 21st century and beyond. All students can and should have access to rigorous instruction and learning. (pp. 17–18)

Lending to the confusion about what is rigor is the word's definition found in dictionaries. Most dictionaries will define rigor with words like "severity, rigidity, strictness, harshness, and/or hardship," which seems counter to the kind of climate educators envision for school. We also see the term, rigor, associated with rigor mortis (the stiffening of the body after death). As we observe many of our nation's schools, we already see too many students bored to death. Is additional boredom the goal of the quest for rigor in our classrooms?

Using a conceptually erroneous definition may be what leads teachers to infuse endless repetition, long hours filling out worksheets, and irrelevant assignment with the thought that more is synonymous to rigor. The end result may be more boredom for our students. If we want to achieve the objectives associated with rigorous teaching, we must understand the concept of rigor. Schools and school leaders can't incorporate more into or determine the presence of rigor into their instruction without an understanding of rigor.

Strong, Silver, and Perini (2001) state, "Rigor is the goal of helping students develop the capacity to understand content that is complex, ambiguous, provocative, and personally or emotionally challenging" (p. 7). Washor and Mojkowski (2006/2007) define rigor as deep immersion in a subject that should include real-world setting and working with experts. Wagner (2008b) in defining rigor says it includes a focus on skills for life: critical thinking and problem solving, collaboration and leadership, agility and adaptability, initiative and entrepreneurialism, effective oral and written communication, accessing and analyzing information, and curiosity and imagination.

Blackburn and Williamson (2009) assert that "true rigor is creating an environment in which each student is expected to learn at high levels, each student is supported so he or she can learn at high levels, and each student demonstrates learning at a high level" (p. 2). They add, "Only when you create a culture of high expectations and provide support so students can truly demonstrate understanding [do] you have a rigorous classroom" (p. 2). Blackburn in a blog, *Response: Thoughts on the Meaning of "Rigor"* (Ferlozzo, 2012), expounds on the definition of rigor and notes four key aspects of rigor:

- Rigor requires the creation of an environment that leads to growth. Rigor doesn't happen overnight; it is a process. If students are making small steps, that means there is student growth. Celebrating that growth and encouraging students to not give up and to do better will lead to an environment that supports rigor.
- Rigor requires a high expectations focus for students. High expectations is not just a belief, it is a behavior that supports high student achievement, one that eliminates the word "can't" from the minds and behaviors of both students and educators.
- Rigor requires providing support for students so they can master skills at higher levels; thus, scaffolding within a lesson is imperative. Additional ways to provide student support are to create strategies to mold student thinking processes and close achievement gaps, and to provide students help outside of class time that need it.
- Rigor requires each student to demonstrate their understanding of acquired knowledge mastery of skills. Art activities, writing experiences, and projects are excellent way for students to individually demonstrate what they know. During whole group instruction the use of clickers, thumps-up thumps-down strategies, and think-pair-shares are excellent ways to monitor each students understanding of each part of the lesson.

Blackburn suggests that we build on what we are already doing, namely, demonstrating high expectation, providing support for students, and asking students to show what they understand; doing so, she asserts, will create a climate that supports rigor. Noting that rigor is more than lesson planning or teaching rigorous standards, she concludes that rigor is an implementation process. It is the weaving together of curriculum, instruction, and assessment in a way that students excel at higher levels.

Tovani (2011) in her book, *So What Do They Really Know*, explains the difference between a rigorous classroom and a hard one in terms of student success. She points out that rigor invites engagement that causes student to lose track of time, while hard repels engagement and causes time to drag. In a rigorous classroom, she notes, students feel encouragement, self-confident, and a sense of accomplishment. In a hard classroom, on the other hand, there is evidence of discouragement, avoidance, disappointment. She believes rigor is not about quantity or rate, but depth. With this in mind, she states that rigor varies from student to student, depending on the skill level of the learner and his or her motivation to succeed. The attainment bar moves as each student progresses.

Jackson (2011) proclaims that "rigor is one of those slippery concepts in education. Everyone agrees that it is important, and everybody wants standards, instruction, and assessments that are rigorous, but very few agree on what 'rigor' really means. In most cases, educators believe that they know rigor when they see it without really having a fully defined idea of what it looks like" (pp. 14–15). She suggests that we "think of the times you might have used the term 'rigorous' to mean a learning task that was 'harder' or 'more challenging' or 'focused on the upper levels of Bloom's taxonomy.' While all of these concepts play into rigor, rigor is more than that. So before we begin the work of this how-to guide—planning rigorous learning units—it is important to define what we mean when we talk about rigor in the classroom" (p. 15).

Citing Resnick (1987) she states that "rigor is a *quality of instruction* that requires students to construct meaning and impose structure on situations rather than expect to find them already apparent" (Resnick, 1987, p. 44). She adds, "Whereas most units work toward what students will know and be able *to do* by the end of instruction, rigorous learning units also ask *what students* will understand and how students will be able to think. Rigorous instruction is designed to develop students' capacity to

- Think accurately and with clarity.
- Identify and consider multiple meanings and interpretations.
- Take and support a position.
- Resist impulsivity and engage in disciplined inquiry and thought.
- Work within and outside the bounds of standard conventions, and develop their own standards of evaluation.
- Use and adapt what they know to deal with uncertainty and novelty.
- Adjust their approach when presented with new constraints.
- Tolerate uncertainty and work through ambiguity and complexity" (p. 15).

Jackson (2011) further explains that rigorous instruction is for every student, not only for selected students in gifted, talented, or honors programs. It is challenging, not difficult; requires more effort, not more work; is related to quality, not related to quantity; is messy and free ranging, not algorithmic, scripted learning; and is possible at all levels of learning, not reserved for the upper levels of Bloom's taxonomy. She concludes, "In short, rigor is quality of instruction that goes beyond helping students memorize facts, acquire an understanding of concepts, and develop basic skill proficiency. Rigorous instruction asks students to create their own meaning, integrate skills into processes, and use what they have learned to solve real-world problems, even when the 'correct' answer is unclear and they are faced with perplexing unknowns" (p. 15).

Socol (Ferlozzo, 2012), a "Senior Provocateur" with Band of Educators, is critical of the term rigor that has overshadowed education. He writes:

There is a reason revolutions bring new vocabularies. Language is a powerful thing, and trying to describe how you or your idea is different from what came before, though it has the same name, is difficult. Napoleon and Washington did not call themselves "King," a loaded word. "Automobile" and "car" trumped "horseless carriage" for the same reason. But here we are in education with the word "rigor." You know, "rigor," from Old French: "stiffness, rigidness, rigor, cold, harshness, difficult." We have a word which describes something few educators actually want, but because politicians like the word, we waste unbelievable energy trying to redefine it.

For "all" students to succeed, we need no "rigor" at all, we need the opposite: flexible. adaptive. active. communicative. collaborative. We need *Universal Design* (joining together of differentiated instruction, new information and communication technologies, and learner-directed education) in our classes and *tool-belts* (as humans picking tools based on the task at hand) in our students' hands, so they can reach the necessary learning—now millions of times greater than just a generation ago—as efficiently and effectively as they can.

So please stop trying to re-define a word which represents something we do not want. Instead, let us say what we mean as we fight to re-imagine education. (Socol, 2012)

Kovacs (Socol, 2012), a columnist for EdNews.org, suggests we replace rigor with vigor. He asks us to consider some definitions for vigor: active strength or force, healthy, physical or mental energy or power, vitality, energetic activity, energy, intensity. He further asks us to consider some of vigor's synonyms: drive, strength, force, flourish, vitality. He concludes that vigor sounds far more descriptive of engaging and purposeful learning environment than the term rigor. But Socol (2012) says he is tired of buzzwords and doesn't want to pick a replacement for "rigor" from a rhyming dictionary. Instead, what he wants is an understanding of what educational opportunity means. He believes that "real" education helps students to develop the capacity to understand content that is *complex, ambiguous, provocative, personally or emotionally challenging, active, deep, and engaging*. He illustrates each with questions:

> *Complex and deep.* What is the difference between mapping John Smith's journey to Virginia on an outline map (the fifth grade history curriculum for these kids next fall) and knowing what the Quay in Southampton looks like? *Provocative.* What happens when children attending what was once a "Colored School" (by law) discover that in Belfast discrimination like that happens among white people? *Personally or emotionally challenging.* What to make of the story of a twelve-year-old living on his own, when you are nine? *Ambiguous.* Could this story be true? Does it make sense? *Active and engaging.* Well, yes it was. (Socol, 2012)

Addressing what she sees as the real purpose of rigor, Schutz (2007) stresses that rigor is the use of instructional delivery methods similar to project-based instruction, which uses an inquiry model that empowers students to seek their own answers to important issues, create models that represent their findings, and explore ways their discoveries can make a positive difference in the world. Rigor, she adds, is about educators finding ways to connect classrooms to the world and to help create those personal and emotional synapses that motivate students to embrace challenging curriculum. It is about classrooms, she concludes, where students are taught the strategies needed to attack challenging text, detect bias, gather relevant information, and use what they've learned to work in a useful and meaningful way.

Whether it is rigor, vigor, or term-less, it is now time, past time, to change the dull, hum-drum instruction that we find in too many American classrooms, to create wonderful, exciting, and inviting classrooms where students succeed, are engaged, and are challenged. To engage our youth in active, stimulating, thought-provoking learning, instead of the "schooling" believed caused by the testing craze. It is time to have high expectations for all of our students exhibited by our classroom instruction. It has to be more than a saying, "All children can learn." Teaching is an art, a craft, a science. American schools do not need any more Teach for America's untrained teachers or Arne Duncan's Kipp Academies with training in staring and chanting (Socol, 2012). Finally, if we are to create the desired classroom with the desired level of instruction, educational leaders must step up and deliver instructional leadership.

HIGH EXPECTATIONS AND RIGOR

In the heart of rigor are high expectations for all students. Blackburn (2013) states that rigor is creating an environment in which each student is expected to learn at high levels. To do this the staff must believe and, more so, demonstrate that all students can attain mastery of the essential skills and that they have the capability to help all students achieve mastery. Edmonds (1979) made a profound statement that seems, decades later, to be unfortunately true. He noted, "Schools teach those they think they must[,] and when they think they needn't[,] they [do not]" (p. 16). He also is noted for saying, " There has never been a time in the life of the American public school when we have not known all we needed to in order to teach all those whom we chose to teach" (p. 19). Having high expectations starts with the decision that every student possesses the potential to be his or her best, no matter what. Benard (1995), in addressing the value of high expectations in schools, notes that schools that establish high expectations for all students and provide the necessary support to achieve academic success.

Lezotte (1991) notes that in the first generation of effective school research, "teachers found themselves in the difficult position of having had high expectations and having acted upon them—yet some students still did not learn" (p. 2). Today in the second generation he suggests that it is necessary for teachers to anticipate this and develop a broader array of responses. "For example, teachers will implement additional strategies, such as reteaching and regrouping, to assure that all students do achieve mastery. Implementing this expanded concept of high expectations will require the school as an organization to reflect high expectations. Most of the useful strategies will require the cooperation of the school as a whole; teachers cannot implement most of these strategies working alone in isolated classrooms" (p. 2). He asserts:

> High expectations for success will be judged, not only by the initial staff beliefs and behaviors, but also by the organization's response when some students do not learn. For example, if the teacher plans a lesson, delivers that lesson, assesses learning and finds that some students did not learn, and still goes on to the next lesson, then that teacher didn't expect the students to learn in the first place. If the school condones through silence that teacher's behavior, it apparently does not expect the students to learn, or the teacher to teach these students. Several changes are called for in order to implement this expanded concept of high expectations successfully. First, teachers will have to come to recognize that high expectations for student success must be "launched" from a platform of teachers having high expectations for self. Then the school organization will have to be restructured to assure that teachers have access to more "tools" to help them achieve successful learning for all. Third, schools, as cultural organizations, must recognize that schools must be transformed from institutions designed for "instruction" to institutions designed to assure "learning" (pp. 2–3).

Benard (1995) states that there are several ways of conveying positive and high expectations to students. Among them he notes:

- Building personal relationships in which teachers and other staff communicate to students, "This work is important; I know you can do it; I won't give up on you"
- Providing firm guidance, challenge, and stimulus—plus loving support
- Refusing to label their students "at risk"; looking at each child to see the gem that is inside and communicating this vision back to the child
- Grouping students to indicate the expectations we have for them
- Using several assessment approaches, not relying solely on standardized test as a means of evaluation
- Instilling among students the responsibility for and ownership of learning

Thus, conveying high expectations to students means exhibiting a belief and developing in students' self-esteem and self-efficacy. High expectations require your actions to speak louder than your words. In other words, if you want to know what a person really believes, watch his or her actions. This supports Edmonds' (1979) belief of high expectations being a behavior, not just a belief. However, having high expectations is not enough; there is a clear connector between motivation and engagement and achievement. Students respond more positively to high-level expectations when they value what they are doing (Kingore, 2007). Thus, teachers need to know how to make learning in the classroom rigorous and not by just adding additional busy work. This requires teachers to have a knowledge base, technical skills, and interpersonal skills.

HIGHER-ORDER THINKING AND RIGOR

Levin (2004) suggests that in order to effectively prepare students to successfully engage with their environment, we must improve students' higher-order thinking skills. Blackburn (2013) also states that a way to make a classroom more rigorous is for teachers to use questions that are more open-ended, rather than having one single, simple answer. Asking higher-level questions is a key piece of creating the environment that supports increased rigor in the classroom. Teachers have to work on not only asking better questions but also asking questions better. Skilled questioning enables teachers to know what students need to master in their learning, to challenge students' thinking and, to provide scaffolding to support the higher expectations, pushing students' thinking higher or deeper. More often than not, classroom discussions consist of lower-order questions that are answered by a few motivated students.

While lower-level questions should be asked in order to build on them, we should recognize that lower-level questions are not of a quality to provide detailed information about student thinking, and learning and responses are not systematically collected from all students in the class. Tobin and Capie (1982) found the use of higher-order questions, and increased wait time significantly contributed to increases in student engagement (e.g., attending to a task, responding to questions, collecting data, explaining information) and academic achievement. Crooks's (1988) research also supports the use of higher-level questions to actively engage students and increase student achievement. He suggests that directing classroom questions to as many students as possible will lead to greater benefit.

The oldest teaching tactic for fostering critical thinking dates back centuries to Socrates (Vlastos, 1995). In Socratic teaching the focus is on providing questions with questions, not answers (Garlikov, 2006). Socrates (Garlikov, 2006) challenged the "loose" thinking of the youth of his day by asking such questions as: "What is the evidence?" and, "If this is true, does it not follow that certain other matters are true?" (p. 131).

Most educators use the old taxonomies (Bloom, Englehart, Furst, Hill, & Krathwohl, 1956) or Krathwohl's (2002) revision of Bloom's taxonomy as a guide for teachers to raise the level of their questioning. Bloom's taxonomy has multiple levels of higher-order thinking. The Gallagher and Aschner program, like Ciardiello's (1998) Four Types of Questions, has fewer levels and seems more user friendly (Gallaher & Aschner, 1963).

GALLAGHER & ASCHNER CLASSIFICATION MODEL

Gallagher and Aschner (1963) suggest in their research that there is a high correlation with question asking and the development of higher-order thinking skills. They offer an instrument capable of accurately classifying the thought level required of the student by a teacher's question. These researchers developed a four-level model designed to suggest the various kinds of questions teachers use in the classroom. The levels they identified are: (1) cognitive-memory (low-order convergent), (2) convergence (high-order convergent), (3) divergence (low-order divergent), and (4) evaluative (high-order divergent).

There are similarities between the Gallagher and Aschner (1963) model of questioning and the versions of Bloom's taxonomy. Bloom et al. (1956) created a hierarchy of levels of thinking with remembering and recalling as the lowest level. Synthesis (creation) and evaluation were the highest levels of thinking based on the view that students begin with a basic understanding of the content (vocabulary, dates, formulas) and then move to integrate this understanding with prior knowledge eventually creating new conceptualizations. The new version (Krathwohl, 2002) moves from the lowest level of remembering to creating.

The Gallagher and Aschner model evaluates teacher questions by determining if they are higher - or lower-level thinking. In this model, convergent questions, which typically only have one correct answer, are considered a lower level than divergent questions, which have many possible answers and thus invite students to consider several aspects of the question involving more cognitive processes. The model also divides the convergent and divergent questions into levels similar to Bloom et al. where the amount of cognitive processing involved determines whether the question is considered higher or lower level (Gallagher & Aschner, 1963).

GALLAGHER & ASCHNER CLASSIFICATION SCHEME

The first level of the Gallagher and Aschner (1963) questions classification scheme is that of cognitive-memory and is considered the lowest level of thought required of students. Questions at this level demand that students recall, identify-observe, define, name, designate, or respond yes or no. Examples of questions that fall under this category are as follows:

Who is the main character in the story?
What is energy?
What coin is this?
Did the boy give the candy to his friend?
Who was the first character in the book to find the hidden cave?

The second level of the Gallagher and Aschner (1963) questioning system is called convergent. This category includes more broad type of questioning that required putting facts together in order to acquire the right answer but is still considered a low level of the thought. This type calls for students to explain, state relationships, or compare and contrast. Examples of such questions are:

Why does the moon give off light?
How are dogs and cats alike?
What does the mother do when she discovers her ring missing?

The third level of the Gallagher and Aschner (1963) questioning system is considered broad and is called divergent. Divergent questions allow for more than one answer and encourage creative and imaginative responses. Students are required to predict, hypothesize, infer, or reconstruct. Examples are as follows:

If you ruled the world, what would you change?
What do you think the girl will do next?
How would the United States be different if it had lost the American Revolution?
Suppose you were an African American child how would your life be different?

The final category of the Gallagher and Aschner (1963) scheme is called evaluative. The evaluative question is classified as broad and requires the student to judge, value, choose, or defend. The following are examples of these kinds of questions:

Is America the best country within to live and why?
Why did you select this one as the correct one?
Do you agree with the decision of our country to enter the war? Why?

RECOMMENDATIONS FOR THE PRACTICING PRINCIPAL

Many studies (Cawelti, 2000; Haberman, 1999; Jesse, Davis, & Pokorny, 2004; McGee, 2004) identify the principal's leadership as important to a school's high performance. They consistently point to the principal as a key player in sustaining the sense of success for all. Carter (2000) asserts that the presence of a strong principal who holds everyone to the highest standards is the most notable factor in creating a high-performing school. Sparks (2004) supports this assertion: "Skillful teaching in every classroom requires skillful leadership by principals. There are no substitutes" (p. 1).

As agents of change, principals have the opportunity and responsibility to support teachers' use of higher-order thinking in their classrooms. Teachers are the direct influence on student behavior and test performance. Thus, it is imperative that teachers understand and support the use of higher-order thinking. "The teacher is the key figure when it comes to influencing student performance; therefore, teacher professional development programs should focus on improving teaching quality" (Kuijpers, Houtveen, & Wubbels, 2010, p. 1687). It is recommended that principals become familiar with the Gallagher and Aschner four types of questions and then conduct professional development with teachers to share the understanding. Researchers have found that allowing teachers time to develop an understanding to a new method and to communicate with others regarding the change is a significant predictor of positive implementation (Buzhardt, Greenwood, Abbott, & Tapia, 2006).

It is crucial to provide time for professional learning communities to study and practice implementing higher-order thinking strategies. Doing so illustrates the school's commitment to improving the educational process. McComas and Abraham (2004) provide a questionnaire that learning communities of teachers could use to rate their own questioning behavior of students. Bringing awareness to the types of questions used is a first step in helping teachers become mindful of their teaching practice. Teachers could engage in peer observation and simply rate the questions as high/low, divergent/convergent for one another to get a third-party analysis. Teachers could compare initial observation scores with later observations to track implementation success. This process of focusing on the goal, establishing a baseline through the self-report questionnaire, observation, and post observation reflection is based on the Kuijpers et al. (2010) two cycle process for professional development.

The first cycle focuses on individual performance and understanding. The second cycle or tier focuses on the teachers as a team evaluating progress on implementation as a group, practicing the new skills, and comparing data on student achievement or teacher competencies. The two-cycle process requires a time commitment on the part of the teachers and the principal to be successful. Individual teachers should expect to conduct peer observations at least three times in one another's classroom, and student achievement data could take at least one quarter to note any change. The process could even take an academic year as the students and teachers adjust to a new form of teaching practice. The extent to which the principal supports the process will clearly demonstrate the importance of implementing this new teaching strategy.

Following staff development, it is recommended that the principal make classroom visits where the focus is on the levels of questions that a teacher asks. The questions should be ranked and discussed with the teacher during the post-conference. While the inclusion of questions that elicit higher-order thinking is the goal, principals and teachers need to understand that teachers cannot or should not ask only high-level questions. Responses to lower-level questions are used as a foundation for responses to higher-level questions. A thorough understanding needs to be established before students have the necessary skills to engage in higher-level thinking about new content.

CREATING RIGOR IN THE CLASSROOM

Translating the rhetoric about rigor into classroom reality, giving life to it has proven difficult. Blackburn's (2013) nationally recognized concept of instructional rigor includes high expectations, scaffolding for instruction, and demonstration of learning. But she admits that teachers everywhere don't know what it looks like or how to do it. Thus enters the educational leader who as the instructional leader is responsible for professional learning. Effective teaching is not the end; it is the means to an end: student achievement. Instructional leadership is improving instruction in order to increase student learning (Glickman, Gordon, & Ross-Gordon, 2013).

Achieving the goal of improving instruction requires a supportive system, and that supportive system is more important given the confusion surrounding rigor in the classroom. To help Williamson and Blackburn (2011) say when all elements of schooling are weaved together to improve the achievement and learning of every student, we are then able to achieve rigor. Focusing on their identified aspects of rigor (environment, expectations, support, and demonstration), they offer several tools that can be used to develop rigor in the classroom.

The first is a tool to tally teacher questions and responses to students while making classroom observations. The results can be used for discussions during a post-observation phase of a clinical observation process. In rigorous classrooms teachers ask higher-level questions and don't accept low-level responses from students. Instead teachers, using their questioning skills, probe and guide students to give higher-level responses. In rigorous classrooms students are supported so they can learn at higher levels. To achieve this, Williamson and Blackburn suggest the tool of scaffolding. Teachers should seek ways of doing this. Williamson and Blackburn (2011) offer the following examples of scaffolding strategies:

- Asking guiding questions
- Chunking information
- Color-coding the steps of a project
- Writing standards as questions for students to answer
- Using visuals and graphic organizers
- Providing such tools as interactive reading guides and study guide

Here are some additional scaffolding strategies:

- Ask students to share their own experiences, hunches, and ideas about the content or concept of study and have them relate and connect it to their own lives. This strategy motivates or enlists the student's interest related to the task.
- Show or demonstrate to students exactly what they are expected to do. This strategy provides some direction in order to help the child focus on achieving the goal.
- Weave in think-pair-share, turn-and-talk, triad teams, or some other structured talking time throughout the lesson. This strategy defines a shared goal

for all students to achieve through engagement in specific tasks and eliminates students' confusion.
- Use cooperative learning. This strategy creates momentum and decreases student confusion.
- Preteach vocabulary, introducing words to students using pictures and objects, and other ways of tapping into their experiences and interests. Require students to create a symbol or drawing for each word and allow time for discussion of the work. This strategy simplifies the task to make it more manageable and achievable for a child.
- Use graphic organizers, pictures, and charts. This strategy helps students to achieve the goal.
- Use open-ended questions. This strategy creates an environment where students feel safe taking risks and promotes critical thinking. It also gives the teacher an opportunity to monitor growth.
- Use strategic questioning with pause time for students to think and reflect. This strategy leads to efficiency; learning goals are achieved efficiently.

During the classroom observation, principals should look for evidence of scaffolding and discuss their findings with the teacher. If professional development is warranted, it should be provided.

Williamson and Blackburn (2011) note that student engagement is a key aspect of rigor and teachers should provide students opportunities to demonstrate what they have mastered. In the teaching process, teachers normally ask questions and call on one student to respond. To increase student engagement, promote high levels of student accountability, and to give students opportunities to demonstrate learning, a teacher can allow all students to response by using handheld computers, small whiteboards, thumbs up or down, and/or pair-share. They can suggest the tool of student engagement where principal note the negative and positive indicators of student engagement observed during a classroom visitation. Examples of negative indicators are only one student response is sought, or when the teacher asks students do they understand, the students respond yes, and the teacher proceeds with no probing or further questioning. Examples of positive indicators are when teachers have ways for all students to respond, students are allowed to discuss content in small groups, or students respond using journal entries or exit slips.

The last tool offered by Williamson and Blackburn (2011) is the tool of talking with the teacher. Using this tool, principals can discuss with teachers, among other things, how they make a lesson engaging; the information they use to guide their decisions, the strategies they use to make sure the lesson is engaging, the monitoring processes used to ensure student engagement, how they can improve what they are doing, and how the educational leaders in the building can support them in their efforts to improve student engagement.

Blackburn (2008) in her book, *Rigor Is NOT a Four-Letter Word*, devotes five chapters to concrete ways to increase rigor in the classroom. She offers specific strategies that David-Lang (2011) has selected and summarized a few from each chapter:

Ways to Increase Rigor
Raise the level of content
Increase complexity
Give appropriate support
Open your focus
Raise expectations
Raise the level of content

Research has shown that many of our students believe what they are learning is too easy. One girl described her low-level classes as "teaching nothing over and over again." One way to increase the rigor for all students is to raise the level of content. You can do this by:

1. Valuing Depth—We often focus on shallow coverage of many topics. For true rigor, we need students to develop a depth of understanding.
2. Increasing Text Difficulty—An effective way to raise the level of content is to increase the difficulty of the texts the students read.
3. Creating Connections—By creating interdisciplinary units or lessons, you can increase the rigor by providing an opportunity for students to apply the content they have learned in another discipline.
4. Reviewing, Not Repeating—We spend too much time going over basic content. It doesn't work to repeat the same information over again. Instead, we need to find a new and authentic way for students to use basic knowledge as a different way to review.
5. Evaluating Content—We need to raise our expectations for the type of work students produce so that when we require students perform at the "proficient" level, it is actually proficient according to national or other more rigorous standards.

Increase Complexity

Another way to enhance rigor is by increasing the complexity of your assignments. We spend entirely too much time on rote memorization and recitation of facts. Instead, we need to get our students to practice using that information at higher levels and applying that information in new ways. The following are a few suggested ways to do this:

1. Complexity through Projects—For example, rather than simply working on a set of equations to solve for slope, students might also design the ideal roller

coaster—a much more complex and ambiguous problem. Having groups of students solve this problem addresses another facet of complexity—the ownership is shifted to the students. Another key element is to design a rubric that lays out the expectations for higher-order analysis in the project.
2. Complexity in Writing—We often ask our students to perform lower-order thinking when writing. For example, we might ask students to write a paragraph about a topic such as the solar system. Instead, we need to vary the types of writing assignments we give students so they can understand the topic at a higher level.
3. Complexity as You Assess Prior Knowledge—Many teachers assess students' current level of knowledge about a new topic using a K-W-L chart (What do you KNOW, WANT to know, and what have you LEARNED?) Instead, teachers can use a more rigorous way to assess for prior knowledge.
4. Complexity with Vocabulary—Giving your students a routine list of vocabulary words rarely leads to deeper comprehension of meaning. In a rigorous classroom you want students to demonstrate their understanding with more thorough explanations, details, examples, and elaboration.
5. Complexity in Review Games—Teachers often use simple games to review material. To maximize the involvement of students, have the students create the questions from their notes, labs, and so on and enhance the rigor by requiring everyone to respond to each question.

Give Appropriate Support and Guidance

A third way to enhance rigor is to provide the necessary support and scaffolding needed in order for your students to do more challenging work. If you want to raise expectations, you must also provide the accompanying support to help your students meet those expectations or you are setting them up to fail. The following are a few suggested ways to do this:

1. Scaffolding during Reading Activities—Reading is used in almost every classroom and often provides an obstacle for students who struggle with reading skills. This section is not about teaching students how to read but rather provides three strategies to guide students through their reading.
2. Modeling—There are several ways to provide a model to help your students. You can make your thinking explicit by doing a 'think-aloud' when, for example, you talk through what you think when reading a textbook (about the headings, the glossary, etc.). You can also post a written set of procedures on the wall as a model—such as "What to Do When You Don't Know a Vocabulary Word"—that shows what strong readers do when they don't know a new word.

3. Providing Clear Expectations—Students often don't know what quality work looks like. This is especially the case when we go beyond asking them to recite facts and require that they use higher-order thinking skills—such as describing the causes of an event, persuading a reader, or explaining the results of a science experiment. It is important to provide students with a clear checklist of your guidelines, sample pieces of student work that meet and don't meet those guidelines, and opportunities for students to determine whether those samples meet the guidelines.
4. Chunking Big Tasks—To help students tackle larger tasks, break the work into more manageable chunks and provide additional instruction at each step of the way.
5. Presenting Multiple Opportunities to Learn—Not all students learn the material the first time around. As teachers it is our responsibility to provide them with additional opportunities to ensure that they learn. This may mean meeting with a struggling student to expose him or her to the questions or content before class so he or she can be better prepared. Or it may mean requiring students (rather than offering) to meet with you for additional assistance.

Include More Open-Ended Tasks and Questions

The fourth way to make your classroom more rigorous is to find more opportunities to give students open-ended tasks and questions. More rigorous tasks and questions tend to be open-ended rather than having one single, simple answer. Many students can calculate a simple equation, but when the task is embedded in a paragraph that requires them to apply their mathematical knowledge, they have more trouble. This doesn't mean you should ignore the instruction of basic facts; you should just make sure to also focus on the use and application of those facts rather than just asking students to memorize them. The following are a few suggested ways to incorporate more open-ended tasks and questions:

1. Open-Ended Questioning—As you write questions for your lessons, it is important to incorporate questions that have more than one answer because these are usually the higher-order questions. Another way to develop your questioning technique is to push students beyond their initial answers and ask them to follow-up, "How did you know?" "What made you decide on that answer?"
2. Open-Ended Vocabulary Instruction—The traditional method of having students memorize vocabulary words does not result in long-term acquisition of new words. Instead you need to give students the opportunity to experience the new words in different ways, incorporate old knowledge of

words with new, and play with words to develop a deeper understanding of them. One way is to have students write poems about words—like a haiku—to fully capture and express their meaning.
3. Open-Ended Projects—Open-ended projects allow students to delve more deeply into the material. One way to do this is to have students complete an assignment from different points of view. For example, in science, have students write about a drug to cure a deadly illness from the perspectives of the drug company as well as the patient who needs the cure.
4. Open-Ended Choices for Students—If you provide students with more choices in an assignment, then students will invest more time and effort into the task. Of course, this does not mean allowing students to do whatever they want, but rather to choose from a few well-structured choices provided by the teacher.
5. Open-Ended from the Beginning—In the United States we tend to teach students something and then have them apply it to a real-world situation. In Japan teachers often start a mathematics class with a problem students do not yet know how to solve, but they let the students struggle with it. Students work alone or in groups, and as they do so, they uncover the important mathematical concepts and reasoning. For example, students might be given materials (toothpicks, glue) and a budget and have to build the strongest bridge possible before being taught the mathematical principles necessary to do so.

Raise Expectations

The final way to increase the rigor in the classroom is to raise expectations—a necessary part of many of the strategies that have already been discussed. The following are five ways to raise expectations:

1. Expect the Best—It is difficult to expect the best from students when their actions tend to make us think less of them. Instead, we need to emphasize the types of teacher behaviors that show all students we expect the best. This means exemplifying the belief that all students can succeed, encouraging students, supporting students, and giving students the time and resources to succeed.
2. Expand the Vision—Many students do not believe they can be successful, and we need to help them expand their visions. Students who have dreams and goals of their own are more likely to put in the effort to succeed.
3. Learning Is Not Optional—When we give students a zero for not doing homework or a D on an assignment rather than asking them to do a more satisfactory job, we are sending the message, "You don't have to learn

this." Rigor is not just raising the bar; it is ensuring that students do the work.
4. Track Progress—As you increase your expectations students need to see that they are making progress in order to maintain their motivation. You can have students keep track of their progress weekly with a journal, chart, or some other way to have them reflect on their progress.
5. Create a Culture of High Expectations—It takes time, but by consistently telling students they are not allowed to say "I can't," building students' confidence, having students track their progress, posting motivating quotations, bringing in role models, and talking about dreams and successes, you will slowly build a culture of high expectations. (David-Lang, 2011, pp. 2–6. Reprinted with permission by Jenn David- Lang of the Main Idea)

Daggett (2008/2014) asserts that "a rigorous and relevant education is a product of effective learning, which takes place when standards, curriculum, instruction, and assessment interrelate and reinforce each other" (p. 2) (Figure 6.1). He adds that "all educators can use the Rigor/Relevance Framework to set their own standards of excellence as well as to plan the objectives they wish to

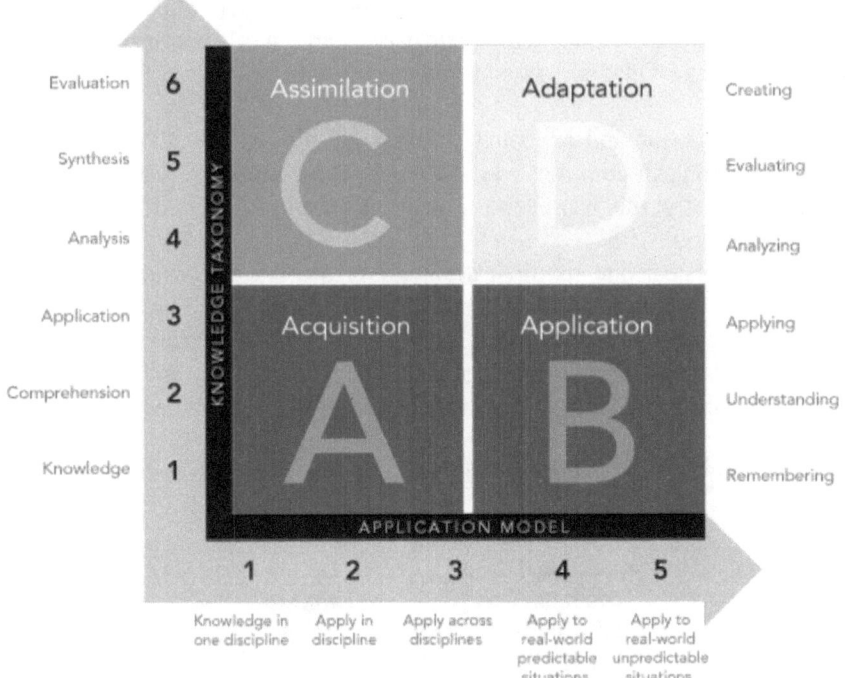

Figure 6.1. International Center for Leadership in Education. Reprinted with permission.

achieve. This versatile framework applies to standards, curriculum, instruction, and assessment.

When planning a lesson using the Rigor/Relevance Framework, it is important to maintain a consistent level of rigor and relevance. For example, if a teacher has lofty curriculum objectives in Quadrant D but develops instruction and test questions that are in Quadrant A, it is unlikely that students will reach the teacher's high expectations. Similarly, if a teacher designs high-rigor instructional activities but uses a low-rigor assessment tool, the test will not be an accurate measure of what students have learned.

When implementing the Rigor/Relevance Framework in a classroom, school, district, or state, it is of great importance to design instruction and develop assessments that measure Quadrant D skills. This enables students not only to gain knowledge but also to develop skills such as inquiry, investigation, and experimentation.

In thinking about ways to incorporate the Rigor/Relevance Framework in instruction and assessment, it is helpful to consider the roles that students and teachers take. When instruction and expected student learning is in Quadrant A, the focus is on teacher work. Teachers expend energy to create and assess learning activities—providing lesson content, creating worksheets, and grading student work. In this scenario the student becomes a passive learner.

When instruction and expected learning moves to Quadrant B, the emphasis is on the student doing real-world work. This work involves more real-world tasks than Quadrant A and generally takes more time for students to complete.

When instruction and expected learning fall in Quadrant C, the student is required to think in complex ways—to analyze, compare, create, and evaluate. Traditionally, this has been the level of learning that students graduated from high school with.

Quadrant D learning requires the student to think and work. Roles have shifted from teacher-centered instruction in Quadrant A to student-centered learning. Quadrant D requires that students understand the standard or benchmark being taught thoroughly, but equally important, they must also understand and conceptualize relevant applications for the content being covered (pp. 3–4).

To further help us understand rigorous instruction, consider this narrative shared by Socol (2012):

> Let me talk about "expecting the most." In early December, in a school in one of those "most at risk" communities in America, I worked with a class of 25 or 26 fourth graders. Not a tiny class. Not kids who come from families with college educated parents. Not kids with computers or broadband at home. Not kids—often—with family food money. These are kids who people often do not expect

much of. The kind of kids Teach for America thinks need untrained teachers. The kind of kids Arne Duncan thinks need KIPP Academies with training in staring and chanting.

We decided to try and teach these fourth graders to effectively multitask. So as the school's librarian read Titanicat, a book about the Titanic which takes place in Belfast and Southampton, I played on an Interactive White Board bringing up maps, and the students, armed with 15 new MacBook Airs (we had 20, but I held 5 back to encourage sharing and cooperation instead of 1:1 individualism), searched for anything in the story they did not know or didn't understand, or for things the story got them interested in.

It was pretty magical. While neither the kids nor their teacher had any preparation for this, the students were brilliant. "What's Belfast?" I asked, "Where is it?" They all found Belfast, despite my refusal to help them spell it ("I'm not sure how to spell it," I told them, "why don't you try and see what happens?"). "Where is it? What country is it in? I asked. "It says, 'U.K.'" a few yelled. So, "What's 'U.K.' mean?" I asked.

"University of Kentucky," one girl called out. "University of Kentucky?" I asked, "does that make sense?" "Kentucky doesn't have an ocean," a boy said very quietly. I repeated his statement. Quickly, "United Kingdom," came as an answer. "United Kingdom?" I said, "what's that?"

We rolled through the story and all of its places and ideas. Was the United Kingdom in England or England in the United Kingdom? If Belfast was in Ireland, why did it say U.K.? Did they still build ships in Belfast? Where, exactly, is Southampton? Didn't the founders of Jamestown, Virginia also sail from there? Why didn't ships sail from London? Why did they sail across the ocean? Were there airplanes in 1912?

The students raced through searches, finding movies old (even silent) and new (Leonardo DiCaprio), finding the streets of Southampton, yes, even wandering in Google Maps to find their own school, their own houses. They found pictures of 1912 airplanes. They found other old ships. They found stuff about southern England. And, let me add this, these are children who often have yet to visit their county seat, much less anywhere further.

But they were being pushed, yes, pushed, to engage with the world in terms of expansive space, expansive time, and expansive ideas, and they weren't resisting, they were leaping forward to engage in this very active learning. And I'll add something else, though none of this directly linked to anyone's curricular content for nine-year-olds, though none of this required long hours of homework to reinforce learning, the kids were high-fiving me in the hall two hours later about how excited they were.

So here was the follow up, and it was for me—the educator—to do. I got back to Michigan and I ordered Titanicat, I Survived the Sinking of the Titanic, 1912, and A Night to Remember and sent all three books, along with digital and audio versions of A Night to Remember, to the school library. Now, if any kids want to go further in investigating this tale, this bit of history, they have both the tools and the opportunity.

This is what we can offer every child. Opportunity and access. We gave these kids something to be excited about which introduced them to other nations, to geography, to science, to history. We gave them the tools with which they could all find ways to research—alone, together, which adult support, whatever each student needed. We gave them the time and the freedom to learn—did all hear the whole story? of course not, half said they got lost in what they were doing. Was that wrong? of course not, I simply said that this kind of "multitasking," knowing how to find out what you didn't know as you read or listened, was something we all need to get better at, because we have to do it all the time. They even had ideas about getting better, "we have to be quieter when we search," more than one child said. (Socol, 2012, reprinted with permission)

MESSAGE FOR THE EDUCATIONAL LEADER

Whether we like or dislike the term rigor or think the whirlwind around rigor is an overkill in this age of accountability, hopefully we all can see the need to take action to create in our classrooms the caliber of instruction conceptualized by the term. The research is there: our nation' classrooms need to be more engaging, intellectually stimulating, challenging, and vigorous. Effective instruction matters. Recognizing the challenge before us is easy, but identifying and infusing the most effective ways into instructional practices to a degree that they become institutionalized is not.

Daggett (2011) reminds us that teaching is more effective when it is effectively supported. Professional learning should be driven by instructional needs, and research and classroom observations indicate the need to assist teachers with the delivery of rigorous instruction. Educational leadership should be focused on improving instruction in order to ultimately increase student achievement. With the uneasiness and the lack of preparation being expressed by teachers, educational leaders must step up and provide the leadership necessary to assist teachers to not only deliver but also master rigorous instruction. As the educational leader you must exhibit patience and be prepared to deal with the resistance from teachers, students, and parents who rebel in the process.

David-Lang (2011) addresses the role of the school leader in enhancing rigor. Here are his suggestions:

In addition to providing PD to teachers on the topic of rigor, it is up to the school leader to emphasize the importance of rigor throughout the year. A few ideas to help you with this task:

1. When you pop into classes, observe for rigor. Use a simple checklist based on the definition of rigor your school has adopted. For example (if you use Blackburn's definition):

- Does the teacher show that s/he holds high expectations for all students? Is the teacher persistent in making sure learning is NOT optional?
- Does the teacher provide the type of support and scaffolding to ensure each student learns? Does the teacher use a variety of approaches to ensure that students are supported to learn at high levels despite their current level?
- How do students demonstrate higher-order thinking? Does the teacher use higher-order questions?

2. When reviewing lesson or unit plans, give feedback about other ways rigor can be enhanced.
3. Make sure teachers have the time they need to discuss rigor during faculty or team meetings, to observe each other for rigor, and to get feedback from the instructional leaders about their success with incorporating rigor.
4. Use observations to determine which aspects of rigor teachers continue to struggle with and plan PD accordingly.
5. Celebrate and share stories of teachers successfully enhancing rigor and students demonstrating learning at higher levels. (p. 9)

Keep in mind that what is inspected is respected. With this thought in mind, it is believed that it is imperative that principals focus on rigor while making classroom observations. The following is a tool created for this purpose (table 6.1):

Table 6.1. Classroom Visitations—Evidence of Rigor in Classroom

Indicators	Evidence
The teacher encourages students to apply new information in several different contexts such as the following: Draw a chart explaining the new information; draw a picture that depicts a scene from the story; develop games utilizing information provided; draw a picture that depicts the main idea of the story; make a cartoon strip showing the main events in the story; create and perform a skit based on the story; write a letter to one of the characters; create a time line for the events in the story; write a short story using the characters in the story with a different ending; write a poem about a scene in the story or one of the characters; create a rap using the new information; create a chart explaining the new information; write and perform a puppet show based on the story; write about your feelings about a character, a scene from the story, or after reading the story.	

(Continued)

Table 6.1. Continued

Indicators	Evidence
The teacher uses cooperative learning and various grouping strategies such as moving from the whole class to groups to pairing and then to independent work and the reverse moving from independent work to pairing and then to groups and the whole class	
The teacher requires students to demonstrate learning via interactive strategies such as thumbs up/ thumbs down, clickers, response cards, etc.	
Students spend time discussing and/or writing about what they are learning.	
Students are engaged such as taking notes and asking questions.	
The teacher uses open-ended assessments and requires a demonstration of comprehension and reflection.	
The teacher welcomes students' opinions and ideas into the flow of the lesson.	
The teacher uses noncontrolling language with the class.	
The teacher requires students to use journals to record what they learn.	
Students explain what they are learning and the relevance of what they are learning.	
The teacher requires student work to be revised and improved for mastery.	
The teacher allows wait time—time for the student to think before answering.	
The teacher requires students to expound on and defend their answers.	
The teacher uses incorrect and superficial answers to build upon; they are accepted, but the teacher uses questioning strategies to develop answers.	
The teacher uses open-ended questions that require students to think at higher levels, analyzing cause and effect, predicting outcomes and supporting their predictions, synthesizing information to draw original conclusions, extending their learning by connecting it to other learning, etc.	
The teacher requires students to explain and defend their answers.	
When a student cannot answer a question and another student can, the teacher returns to the first student for the answer. The process is continued until the original student gives the correct answer.	

Indicators	Evidence
The teacher requires students to analyze reading materials.	
When students are not specific and use terms like "you know," the teacher prods for thorough responses.	
The teacher allows or encourages students to utilize technologies to complete assignments, conducting research using the Internet, using word processors, databases, and spreadsheets to organize and report their thinking, using graphing calculators to help them conceptualize, etc.	
The teacher provides dictionaries and other supportive sources and encourages students to use academic and specific vocabulary.	
The teacher does not short-circuit learning by solving problems; instead the teacher provides students with strategies they can use and let them solve problems.	
The teacher requires students to identify and examine similarities and differences.	
The teacher uses higher-level questions.	
The teacher calls on *all* students for responses, not just the better performing students.	

Final comment: Rigor is philosophical and conceptual in nature. It is rooted in a belief. Achieving rigor in the classroom requires a knowledge base and technical skills to deliver or achieve it in instruction.

REFERENCES

Benard, B. (1995). Fostering resiliency in urban schools. In B. Williams (Ed.), *Closing the achievement gap: A vision to guide change in beliefs and practice*. Oak Brook, IL: Research for Better Schools and North Central Regional Educational Laboratory.

Blackburn, B. *7 myths about rigor in the classroom*. Retrieved April 1, 2015, from http://www.teachthought.com/learning/7-myths-about-rigor-in-the-classroom/

Blackburn, B. (2008). *Rigor is not a four letter word*. Larchmont, NY: Eye on Education, Inc.

Blackburn, B. (2013). *Rigor is not a four letter word*. New York: Routledge.

Blackburn, B. R., & Williamson, R. (2009, November). The characteristics of a rigorous classroom. *Instructional Leader, 22*(6), 1–3.

Bloom, B., Englehart, M., Furst, E., Hill, W., & Krathwohl, D. (1956). *Taxonomy of educational objectives: The classification of educational goals. Handbook I: Cognitive domain*. New York; Toronto: Longmans, Green.

Buzhardt, J., Greenwood, C. R., Abbott, M., & Tapia, Y. (2006). Research on scaling up evidence-based instructional practice: Developing a sensitive measure of the rate of implementation. *Educational Technology, Research, and Development 54*(5), 467–492.

Carnoy, M., & Loeb, S. (2002). Does external accountability affect student outcomes? A cross-state analysis. *Educational Evaluation and Policy Analysis, 24*(4), 305–331.

Carter, S. C. (2000). *No excuses: Lessons from 21 high performing, high-poverty schools*. Washington, DC: Heritage Foundation.

Cawelti, G. (2000). Portrait of a benchmark school. *Educational Leadership*. Arlington, VA: Association for Supervision and Curriculum Development.

Ciardiello, A. (1998). Did you ask a good question today? Alternative cognitive and metacognitive strategies. *Journal of Adolescent & Adult Literacy, 42*, 210–219.

Colvin, R. L., & Jacobs, J. *Rigor: It's all the rage, but what does it mean?* Retrieved April 2, 2015, from http://hechingerreport.org/rigor

Crooks, T. J. (1988). The impact of classroom evaluation practices on students. *Review of Educational Research, 58*(4), 438–481.

Daggett, W. R. (2008/2014). *Achieving academic excellence through rigor and relevance*. International Center for Leadership in Education.

Daggett, W. R. (2011). *The Daggett System for effective instruction: Where research and best practices meet*. Boston: International Center for Leadership in Education.

David-Lang, J. (2011). *The main idea—Current education book summaries: Rigor is not a four-letter word* (Blackburn, B. R. author). Retrieved March 7, 2015, from http://www.themainidea.net/tmi_pdfs2/The%20Main%20Idea%20--%20Rigor%20is%20NOT%20a%20Four-Letter%20Word%20--%20July,%202011.pdf

Dee, T. S., & Jacob, B. (2011). The impact of No Child Left Behind on student achievement. *Journal of Policy Analysis and Management, 30*(3), 418–446.

Edmonds, R. (1979). Effective schools for the urban poor. *Educational Leadership, 37*, 15–24.

Ferlozzo, L. (March 6, 2012*).* Response: Thoughts on the meaning of "rigor." Retrieved March 6, 2015, from http://blogs.edweek.org/teachers/classroom_qa_with_larry_ferlazzo/2012/03/response_thoughts_on_the_meaning_of_rigor.html

Gallagher, J., & Aschner, M. J. (1963). A preliminary report on analysis of classroom interaction. *Merrill-Palmer Quarterly of Behavior and Development, 9*, 183–194.

Garlikov, R. *The Socratic method: Teaching by asking instead of telling*. Retrieved April 2, 2015, from http://www.garlikov.com/teaching/smmore.htm

Glickman, C. D., Gordon, S. P., & Ross-Gordon, J. M. (2013). *Supervision and instructional leadership: A developmental approach*. New York: Pearson.

Gojak, L. *What is all of this talk about rigor*. Retrieved April 5, 2015, from http://www.nctm.org/News-and-Calendar/Messages-from-the-President/Archive/Linda-M_-Gojak/What_s-All-This-Talk-about-Rigor_

Haberman, M. (1999). Victory at Buffalo Creek: What makes a school serving low-income Hispanic children successful? *Instructional Leader, 12*(2). Austin, TX: Texas Elementary Principals and Supervisors Association.

Hanushek, E. A., & Raymond, M. E. (2004). The effect of school accountability systems on the level and distribution of student achievement. *Journal of the European Economic Association, 2*(2–3), 406–415.

Hanushek, E. A., & Raymond, M. E. (2005). Does school accountability lead to improved student performance? *Journal of Policy Analysis and Management, 24*(2), 297–327.

Jackson, R. (2011). *How to plan rigorous instruction.* Alexandria, VA: ASCD.

Jesse, D., Davis, A., & Pokorny, N. (2004). High-achieving middle schools for Latino students in poverty. *Journal of Education for Students Placed at Risk, 9*(1), 23–45.

Kingore, B. (2007). *Reaching all learners: Making differentiation work.* Austin, TX: Professional Associates Publishing.

Krathwohl, D. R. (2002). A revision of bloom's taxonomy: An overview. *Theory into Practice, 41*(4), 212–218.

Kuijpers, J. M., Houtveen, A.A.M., & Wubbels, T. (2010). An integrated professional development model for effective teaching. *Teaching and Teacher Education, 26,* 1687–1694.

Lee, J., & Reeves, T. (2012). Revisiting the impact of NCLB high-stakes school accountability, capacity, and resources: State NAEP 1990–2009 reading and math achievement gaps and trends. *Educational Evaluation and Policy Analysis, 34*(2), 209–231.

Levin, H. M. & Seymour, M. (2004). Educating for humanity: Rethinking the purposes of education: London: Paradigm Publishers.

Lezotte, L. W. (1991). *Correlates of effective schools: The first and second generation.* Okemos, MI: Effective Schools Products, Ltd.

McComas, W. F., & Abraham, L. (2004). *Asking More Effective Questions,* 1–16. Retrieved on March 2, 2016 from https://uwaterloo.ca/centre-for-teaching-excellence/sites/ca.centre-for-teaching-excellence/files/uploads/files/asking_better_questions.pdf

McGee, G. W. (2004). Closing the achievement gap: Lessons from Illinois' golden spike high-poverty high performing schools. *Journal of Education for Students Placed at Risk, 9*(2), 97–125.

Noblit, G. W. (1993). Power and caring. *American Educational Research Journal, 30,* 23–38.

Peterson, P. E., Barrows, S. & Gift, T. (Summer, 2016). After Common Care, states set rigorous standards. Retrieved on December 27, 2017 from: Web site: Http://educationnext.org/after-common-core-states-set-rigorous-standards/

Resnick, L. (1987). *Education and learning to think.* Washington, DC: National Academy Press.

Rogers, D. (1994). Conceptions of caring in a fourth-grade classroom. In A. R. Prillaman, D. J. Eaker, & D. M. Dendrick (Eds.), *The tapestry of caring: Education as nurturance.* Norwood, NJ: Ablex.

Shults, D. (2007). *Is it rigor? Or is it something else?* Retrieved April 5, 2016, from http://debbieshultsblog.blogspot.com/2007/09/is-it-rigor-or-is-it-something-else.html

Socol, I. D. (2012). *Changing gears 2012: Re-thinking rigor.* Retrieved January 3, 2012, from http://speedchange.blogspot.com/2012/01/changing-gears-2012-re-thinking-rigor.html

Sparks, D. (2004). The principal's essential role as a learning leader. *Results.* Exford, OH: National Staff Development Council.

Strong, R. W., Silver, H. J., & Perini, M. J. (2001). *Teaching what matters most: Standards and strategies for raising student achievement.* Washington, DC: Association for Supervision and Curriculum Development.

Tobin, K., & Capie, W. (1982). Relationships between classroom process variables and middle school science achievement. *Journal of Educational Psychology, 74*, 441–454.
Tovani, C. (2011) *So what do they really know*. Portland, ME: Stenhouse Publishers.
Vatterott, C. (2009). *Rethinking homework: Best practices that support diverse needs*. Alexandria, VA: Association for Supervision and Curriculum Development.
Vlastos, G. (1995). *Socratic studies*. Cambridge: Cambridge University Press.
Wagner, T. (2008a). *The global achievement gap: Why even our best schools don't teach the new survival skills our children need—and what we can do about it*. New York: Basic Books.
Wagner, T. (2008b). Rigor redefined. *Educational Leadership, 66*(2), 20–24.
Washor, E., & Mojkowski, C. (2006/2007). What do you mean by rigor? *Educational Leadership, 64*, 84–87.
Wei, X. (2012). Are more stringent NCLB state accountability systems associated with better student outcomes? An analysis of NAEP results across states. *Educational Policy, 26*(2), 268–308.
Williamson, R., & Blackburn, B. (2011). *Recognizing rigor in classrooms: Four tools for school leaders*. Retrieved June 1, 2015, from https://www.google.com/search?ei=jK5JWqCOFcnTjwSyuZ34BA&q=williamson+and+blackburn+2011+recognizing+rigor+in+classrooms%3A+four+tools+for+school+leaders&oq=williamson+and+blackburn+2011+recognizing+rigor+in+classrooms%3A+four+tools+for+school+leaders&gs_l=psy-ab.3...20868.42859.0.43657.53.42.11.0.0.0.208.3985.29j12j1.42.0....0...1c.1.64.psy-ab..0.0.0....0.rTxUyPGNaVE
Wong, M., Cook, T. D., & Steiner, P. M. (2011). No Child Left Behind: An interim evaluation of its effects on learning using two interrupted time series each with its own non-equivalent comparison series (WP-09–11). *Institute for Policy Research Working Paper Series*. Evanston, IL: Northwestern University.

Chapter 7

Engaging Parents for School Success

> We get more touchdowns when all of the players are moving in the same direction.

During the first generation of effective schooling research parent/community support and involvement was not listed among the correlates of effective schooling. Lezotte (1999) notes, "During the first generation, the role of parents in the education of their children was always somewhat unclear. Schools often gave 'lip service' to having parents more actively involved in the schooling of their children. Unfortunately, when pressed, many educators were willing to admit that they really did not know how to deal effectively with increased levels of parent involvement in the schools" (p. 5). However, during the second generation, he stresses that the relationship between parents and the school must be an authentic partnership between the school and home.

Lezotte adds, "In the past when teachers said they wanted more parent involvement, more often than not they were looking for unqualified support from parents. Many teachers believed that parents, if they truly valued education, knew how to get their children to behave in the ways that the school desired. It is now clear to both teachers and parents that the parent involvement issue is not that simple.

Parents are often as perplexed as the teachers about the best way to inspire students to learn what the school teaches. The best hope for effectively confronting the problem—and not each other—is to build enough trust and enough communication to realize that both teachers and parents have the same goal—an effective school and home for all children" (p. 5)! While it was assumed in the first generation that parents understood the need to support the school's mission and, if given the opportunity, would play an important role in helping the school to achieve its mission, today we would be naïve to assume this; instead, in this age of accountability, an effective educational leader needs a well-developed plan to gain the support of the school's academic program and involvement in the school's quest for academic excellence.

THE IMPORTANCE OF PARENTAL SUPPORT AND INVOLVEMENT

"When schools, families, and community groups work together to support learning, children tend to do better in school, stay in school longer, and like school more" (p. 7). This is the conclusion of Henderson and Mapp (2000), authors of *A New Wave of Evidence*, a report from Southwest Educational Development Laboratory that is supported by an overwhelming growing body of research. Gordon's (1979) research indicates that the more comprehensive and long lasting the parent involvement, the more effective it is likely to be, not just on children's achievement, but in the quality of schools as institutions serving the community. Kellaghan, Sloane, Alvarez, and Bloom (1993) reviewed a large body of research and found that the home environment is a powerful factor in determining the academic success of students—their level of achievement, their interest in learning, and the years of schooling they will complete.

According to Henderson and Berla (1994), "The most accurate predictor of a student's achievement in school is not income or social status but the extent to which that student's family is able to: (1) Create a home environment that encourages learning, (2) Express high (but not unrealistic) expectations for their children's achievement and future careers, and (3) Become involved in their children's education at school and in the community" (p. 160). In a study of students from sixty-two African American families between grades five and six it was found that a combination of parental involvement at home and supports at school had a significant positive effect on student grades (Gutman & Midgley, 2000). Moore, Bagin, and Gallagher (2016) conclude, "The bottom line . . . is to help students learn better, and they learn better if parents are involved" (p. 114). They add that this calls for the "partnership concept."

In spite of the research that convincingly underscores the value of parental support and the involvement of parents in the education process, it is a common practice for some educational leaders and teachers to oppose the "partnership concept" (Moore et al., 2016) in an age when parent partnership is more warranted. They fear a turf battle where parents and other community leaders may encroach upon their rights, authority, and duties. Often they question if parents are qualified to know or decide what is best or educationally sound for their children. They fear that most parents do not have the knowledge base or technical expertise to be meaningfully involved in decision making involving curriculum and instruction.

The truth of the matter is that parents can be a valuable resource and are qualified to make suggestions to direct the course of instruction toward excellence. Many parents are excellent problem solvers. They are rich in ideas; and they are skilled in fine-tuning the technical details of ideas or strategies proposed by professionally trained educators. Those educational leaders who have overcome turf battles and fears know that those schools who involve parents as team members in the quest for academic excellence have more touchdowns.

Olsen and Fuller (2010) taking excerpts from their book, *Home School Relations: Working Successfully with Parents and Families* (2008), outline the following benefits of parental involvement:

Benefits for the Children

- Children tend to achieve more, regardless of ethnic or racial background, socioeconomic status, or parents' education level.
- Children generally achieve better grades, test scores, and attendance.
- Children consistently complete their homework.
- Children have better self-esteem, are more self-disciplined, and show higher aspirations and motivation toward school.
- Children's positive attitude about school often results in improved behavior in school and less suspension for disciplinary reasons.
- Fewer children are being placed in special education and remedial classes.
- Children from diverse cultural backgrounds tend to do better when parents and professionals work together to bridge the gap between the culture at home and the culture in school.
- Junior high and high school students whose parents remain involved usually make better transitions and are less likely to drop out of school.

Benefits for the Parents

- Parents increase their interaction and discussion with their children and are more responsive and sensitive to their children's social, emotional, and intellectual developmental needs.
- Parents are more confident in their parenting and decision-making skills.
- As parents gain more knowledge of child development, there is more use of affection and positive reinforcement and less punishment on their children.
- Parents have a better understanding of the teacher's job and school curriculum.

- When parents are aware of what their children are learning, they are more likely to help when they are requested by teachers to become more involved in their children's learning activities at home.
- Parents' perceptions of the school are improved and there are stronger ties and commitment to the school.
- Parents are more aware of, and become more active regarding, policies that affect their children's education when parents are requested by school to be part of the decision-making team.

Benefits for the Educators

- When schools have a high percentage of involved parents in and out of schools, teachers and principals are more likely to experience higher morale.
- Teachers and principals often earn greater respect for their profession from the parents.
- Consistent parent involvement leads to improved communication and relations between parents, teachers, and administrators.
- Teachers and principals acquire a better understanding of families' cultures and diversity, and they form deeper respect for parents' abilities and time.
- Teachers and principals report an increase in job satisfaction.

Benefits for the School

- Schools that actively involve parents and the community tend to establish better reputations in the community.
- Schools also experience better community support.
- School programs that encourage and involve parents usually do better and have higher quality programs than programs that do not involve parents. (pp. 129–130. *Reprinted with permission from the lead author, Glenn Olsen, Professor Emeritus, University of North Dakota*)

In the quest to create an A+ school, educational leaders must recognize that parental involvement is absolutely essential to student achievement in school and in life. Student learning is enhanced when schools gain parental support and encourage parents to stimulate their children's intellectual development. Student learning is further enhanced when educators involve parents in the process of achieving instructional goals. Parents can be empowered to assist their children if they know the school's academic goals, the curriculum, and strategies to improve student achievement. When students achieve, everyone benefits. As students excel, the school is recognized, the teachers are less stressed, and are appreciated, and parents and other family members on a wholesale basis value education, thus creating a learning community.

WAYS TO INVOLVE AND EMPOWER PARENTS

There are numerous ways of involving parents in the school that will appeal to parents and at the same time often empower parents to assist their children in higher academic achievement. Many of these strategies will bring parents into the school so they become acquainted with teachers and other educators and allow them to learn to take a personal interest in various phases of instruction. The following are some suggested ways:

Special Events Focused on Parents—Donuts with Dad and Muffins with Mom are excellent opportunities to share the school's vision, share and expound upon school goals, and give mini workshops on various subject areas. Scheduling Science Nights, Family Reading Nights, Parent as Teachers Days, Grandparent Days, and so on also provide excellent opportunities to involve parents and other key family members.

Math Workshops for Parents—A series of math workshops designed for parents can assist improving student math achievement. During the workshops leaders can share new math vocabulary, systematic ways to master math facts, fun activities that support math achievement that can be done at home, steps used in problem solving, and so on.

Grade or Class Parent Representatives—Either for each class or grade, elect or appoint a parent representative. These parents or guardians could assist with instruction in the classroom, help grade papers, promote positive relations between the teacher and other parents, assist with communication between parents and the school, and so on.

Parent Advisory Committee—Working with the PTO or the PTA select a small body of parents/guardians who will advise the principal or the school improvement team in making managerial or instructional program decisions. The committee will not have final decision-making power; instead, the committee would be a sounding board for school leaders. When leaders are required to present and defend their ideas before implementing them, they tend to make better decisions.

Summer and School Break Activities—To reduce regression that occurs during summer and other school breaks, create a list of fun activities for parents to use to undergird the school's instructional program.

Home Checklist—Students spend considerably more time at home than at school. Provide parents a checklist of suggested environmental conditions for the home, dos and don'ts, and other positive ways to support learning at home.

Homework Hotlines—Using technology create homework hotlines where parents are kept apprised and informed of class homework assignments and where students can get tutorial assistance with their homework assignments.

Parent Resource Centers—Often in school parents of kindergarten students on a half-day schedule hang around the school until their children are dismissed. Provide them a place to socialize with a TV; however, require them give you 10–15 minutes daily where you can share with them information that is key to your quest for academic excellence for your school. Provide materials on issues of concern to parents, such as child development, special education, health and safety, drug education, community resources, discipline, and so on. In the room include sample textbooks, manipulative activities, and audio and videotapes that can be checked out for home use. If schools personalize their schools to the community where it is located, and enhance the comfort level of those being served, more parents will become involved.

Study or Discussion Groups—Organize times when interested parents can come to the school and dialogue on key school issues, problems, and interests. These groups can also focus on current teaching methods that can use to reinforce instruction at home, helping their children to succeed.

Parental Involvement on Curriculum Committees—The federal government and often many states require parental involvement on curriculum committees. Beyond the mandate level, educators should desire parents to be involved on such committees. Parents can take an active and constructive role in helping to define the philosophy for the school, determining the goals and objectives for the year, and identifying best practices to infuse into school instructional strategies. Parents provide a perspective that when respected provides great enrichment.

School Website—Create a school and include a parent page with links to other sites that are aligned with information that supports the school's educational efforts.

Family Day—Plan a Family Day like the ones done at Daniel Hale Elementary School in Gary, Indiana. It was a successful way of strengthening the ties between students, parents, other family members, and the school, while strengthening school pride as well. The event received national coverage and landed an article and front cover exposure in *Educational Leadership*. For more details visit: http://www.ascd.org/ASCD/pdf/journals/ed_lead/el_198805_smith.pdf

Increased Communication Efforts—Maintain regular communication with parents by sending home weekly folders of student work, monthly calendars of special events, school new papers, class newsletter, and weekend work sheets that students and parents can do together. Encourage teachers to communicate regularly with parents via the phone or e-mails. Communication should not be limited to negative reports.

PTAs /PTOs—Parents can be involved in their children's schools by joining Parent Teacher Associations (PTAs) or Parent Teacher Organizations (PTOs) and get involved in decision making about the educational services their children receive. Almost all schools have a PTA or PTO, but often only a small number of parents are active in these groups. School leaders should work with parent leaders to increase participation.

DADS Program—DAD is a program founded for the Gary Community School Corp. by John Finn, following the 1995 Million Man March. It is a group of men who volunteer their services in all Gary Public Schools. They attend school activities such as PTA/PTO, monitor hallways, provide supervision at sporting events and school programs, and make themselves available whenever needed even before and after school. Schools can replicate this meaningful program.

Parent Conferences—In addition to class parent conference held during a school's Fall Open House, schedule at least quarterly individual student progress report conferences. During these conferences when student progress is not favorable, don't just criticize student performance or present data, but offer constructive ways parents can assist their children to improve their academic performance.

While the suggestions cited here do not represent all the possibilities, hopefully, they can be used to initiate a discussion on ways educational leaders can stimulate involvement of parents in their schools. The two main purposes should be to foster student achievement and build a learning community where all stakeholders are in quest of academic excellence.

THE NEED FOR A SCHOOL-COMMUNITY RELATIONS PLAN

Many educational leaders are not enthusiastic about the involvement of parents in the school improvement efforts, and those who are often approach parental involvement in a hodge podge, helter-skelter method. Moore et al. (2016) stress the need for a plan for effort to be productive. They say, "A plan must be developed. . . . or little will happen" (p. 6). "If building school support is important and if parental involvement is important, then there must be a commitment of time and efforts. If the commitment is not made, chances are little will happen, and different education factions will be able to look back and say, 'we should have made the commitment'" (p. 6). The following is a sample of a school-community relations plan created by a student, Thomas Barlow, in my educational leadership program at Indiana University Northwest. The plan was developed under my supervision and slightly modified by me.

School Community Relations Plan

I. Includes the school demographics including all necessary factors (age, sex, race, educational attainment, and gainful occupation for community and age, sex, race, SES and test results for school).

DEMOGRAPHICS

Morton High School is located in Hammond, Indiana. Hammond, Indiana is located in Lake County on the south end of Lake Michigan. The city was named in honor of George Hammond, the founder of the G.H. Hammond packing and slaughter house. In 2010 Hammond replaced Gary, Indiana as the most populous city in Lake County. Hammond is home to Purdue University Calumet, which is a well-known branch of Purdue University.

The total population in Hammond is 83,048. The community is predominately female who make up 51.2% of the population. Males make up the remaining 48.8%. The percentage of people who are eighteen years or over is 72.7% and those who are sixty-five years and over is 13.0%. The median household income in Hammond is $35,528 compared to the state average of $41,567. The average family size in Hammond is 3.23% of people in the household. The unemployment rate in Hammond is 11%. According to the latest census, 60.6% are in the labor force and 12.0% of the families in Hammond are below the poverty level. The percentage of high school graduates are 39.2% which is above the state average of 37.2%. The percentage of residents who possess an Associate's Degree is 4.5%, which is below the state average of 5.8%. Residents with Bachelor's Degrees make up 8.1% of the population. People with graduate or professional degrees make up only 3.1% of the population in Hammond. There are three major race groups in Hammond. Whites make up 74.8% of the population. The Black/African Americans make up 15.3% of the population. Hispanic/Latino make up 21.0% of the population.

Hammond consists of a relatively average size school district. The School City of Hammond (SCH) contains fourteen k-5 elementary schools alone. In addition, SCH contains two middle schools, two independent high schools, and two middle/high school combinations. Within this corporation of schools, nine are identified as Title One funded schools. The list of those schools includes eight elementary schools and one middle/high school combination. I am currently employed as a Special Education Teacher at Morton High School which is located in the SCH. There are eighty-three certified staff members at Morton High School. We have two administrators, one dean, four counselors, one nurse, one media specialist, and sixty-seven certified instructors. We also have one special education case manager, one special education transition specialist, and one school psychologist.

Morton High School's staff consist of 89% Caucasian; 8% are Black; and 3% are Hispanic. The male staff at Morton High School is represented by 43% of the population. The female staff is represented by 57% of the population. The student population is 1,198. There are 560 female students and 638 male students. The ethnicity breakdown is as follows: approximately 37% of students are Caucasian, 32% are Hispanic, 27% are Black, 2% are Multi-Racial, and 1% are Native American and Asian. A significant number of Morton students come from homes that are financially challenged. Although most parents within the community have high school diplomas, their economic situation is below the national average of median income.

The percentage of students who qualify for free and reduced lunch is 59%. According to the results of the End of Course Assessment (ECA) test in Algebra, 47% of students passed. The percentage of students that passed the ECA in English is 49%.

II. Includes a school vision statement, a definition and the development process

According to Bundy (2008) a vision statement "should be an organization's inspiring view of the future that tells people where you want the school to be, what you want it to become, and what you are working towards" (pp. 3–4). The vision is developed with all stakeholders. Those are the parents, teachers, staff, and community leaders.

Morton High School Vision Statement

Hammond Morton High School encourages, enables, and challenges each student to master basic skills. Each student is a critical thinker, has self-esteem, maintains a strong work ethic, and comprehends his/her importance as a productive citizen in the global community.

> Bundy, A. (2008). How are your library's mission and vision statements? *APLIS*, *21*(1), 3–4

III. Includes a school mission statement

Morton High School Mission Statement

Hammond Morton High School will encourage, enable, and challenge each student to master basic skills, become a critical thinker, gain self-esteem, develop a strong work ethic, and comprehend his/her importance as a productive citizen in the global community.

IV. Includes a school-community relations policy statement with the necessary four parts (reason for adopting the policy; the decision to do something or take some form of action for the reasons stated; the general means to be employed in carrying out the decision; and the delegation of authority for carrying out the policy (Moore et al. 2016, p. 39))

Morton High School strongly believes that parent and community involvement is imperative for student academic achievement. The improvement of parent and community involvement can be done by Morton High Schools willingness to implement an effective community relations plan that details the responsibilities of the parents, community, and school involved.

Morton High School is committed to the development and implementation of an effective communications effort with parents and the community to help improve student academic achievement. This effort will depend on an effective two-way communication with both external and internal audiences. The goal of improving student academic achievement will be obtained by using financial, human, and physical resources.

Authority is hereby delegated to the school improvement team (SIT) to develop and implement a community relations plan that entails the responsibilities of all stakeholders involved while creating public activities that will create a welcoming environment for parents and others in the community.

V. Details the school-community relations needs by stakeholders and reveals the sources of the survey information

Teacher Needs

The needs of teachers were determined through a thorough analysis of force field data derived from anonymous internet-based surveys. The following conclusions were drawn from the data collected:

Teachers need:

1. More times of common prep with co-teachers
2. More involvement by parents
3. Better communication between administration and teachers
4. Better communication of discipline procedures (progressive discipline)
5. Better communication of dress code rules
6. More involvement from community leaders

Parent Needs

The needs of parents were determined through a thorough analysis of force field data derived from anonymous internet-based surveys. The following conclusions were drawn from the data collected:

Parent needs:

1. More opportunities to speak with administration
2. Better communication with teachers before reports are distributed
3. More positive contact with teachers
4. More highly qualified teachers
5. Assistance with helping their children with homework
6. More opportunities to be involved in school activities

STUDENT NEEDS

The needs of students were determined through a thorough analysis of force field data derived from anonymous internet-based surveys. The following conclusions were drawn from the data collected.

Student needs:

1. Diverse curriculum/course selection
2. Increased assistance with homework/classwork
3. Access to more/advanced technology
4. More involvement by counselors with class schedule/scholarship information
5. Opportunities to job shadow entrepreneurs in the community
6. Opportunities to discuss personal problems that interfere with school.

V. *Develops a plan including at least three (3) goal statements aligned with identified needs, correlates at least three (3) objectives to each goal statement, notes strategies that will deliver each objective, and identifies an evaluation tool to measure the completion of each objective.*

Goal #1	Objectives	Strategies	Evaluation
Increase parent involvement in the building and school events	1. Identify the interest of parents in the community	1a. Compile a list of student parent addresses. (administrative staff) 1b. Create a survey poling parent incentive interest. (SIT) 1c. Mail survey to parents. (administrative staff) 1d. Give students the survey to take home. (teachers) 1e. Compile results once. received (SIT)	Survey
	2. Identify previous school activities with the most parent involvement	2a. Schedule meeting with SIT. (Principal) 2b. Compile list of school activities from previous year. (SIT) 2c. Vote on most successful event. (SIT)	Survey Questionnaire

(Continued)

Goal #1	Objectives	Strategies	Evaluation
	3. Promote upcoming school activities to parents	3a. Compile a list of parent addresses. (administrative staff) 3b. Create flyers and Parent letters. (students, SIT) 3c. Mail flyers and letters to parents. 3d. Post upcoming events onto school marquee. (administrative staff)	Survey

Goal #2	Objective	Strategies	Evaluation
Provide students with more opportunities to receive academic assistance.	1. Implement after school tutoring program	1a. Create a sign in list for students who need tutoring (teachers). 1b. Create a volunteer parent letter and distribute by mail and students (SIT and administrative staff). 1c. Create a list of willing volunteers (SIT). 1d. Formulate an after school tutoring schedule (SIT). 1e. State the start of after school tutoring program over the PA system (administrative staff). 1f. Implement after school tutoring program (teachers).	Questionnaires Attendance records of events
	2. Implement morning PLATO lab	2a. Create a list of students who need remediation in Math or English (teachers). 2b. Distribute emails to teachers asking for volunteers to monitor lab (principal). 2c. Compile a list of parents in the community (administrative staff). 2d. Create a parent letter promoting PLATO (SIT). 2e. Distribute letter by mail and students (administrative staff, teachers).	Questionnaires Attendance records of events

Goal #2	Objective	Strategies	Evaluation
		2f. Formulate a schedule (principal).	
		2g. State the start of after school tutoring program over the PA system (administrative staff).	
		8b. Implement morning PLATO lab.	
	3. Implement a Peer mentoring program.	3a. Compile a list of incoming freshman students (administrative staff).	Questionnaires Attendance records of events
		3b. Distribute an email to all teachers informing them about the Peer mentoring program (principal).	
		3c. Create a list of students with great character and GPA (teachers).	
		3d. Compile a list of parents in the community (administrative staff).	
		3e. Create a parent letter promoting Peer Mentoring program (SIT).	
		3f. Distribute letter by mail and students (administrative staff, teachers).	
		3g. Train volunteer/ recommended junior or seniors (Teachers, SIT).	
		3h. Implement peer mentoring plan (teachers, SIT).	

Goal #3	Objective	Strategies	Evaluation
Improve external and internal communications	1. Improve communication with parents	1a. Provide parents with log-in information into the grading computer program of the school (administrative staff).	Survey Questionnaires
		1b. Create report card pick up days for parents (SIT, administration, teachers).	
		1c. Conduct parent-teacher conferences for each student (teachers).	

(Continued)

Goal #3	Objective	Strategies	Evaluation
	2. Improve communication with teachers	2a. Develop a suggestion box to be located in the office (Students, Art Teacher).	Questionnaires Survey
		2b. Plan common planning periods with teachers and co-teacher (Principal).	
		2c. Develop a staff/faculty blog to express what works and what doesn't (Computer Technician/Librarian).	
	3. Improve communication with students	3a. Create Peer Mentoring program (SIT, teachers, administrative staff).	Questionnaires Survey
		3b. Schedule and conduct monthly meetings with Student Counsel (principal).	
		3c. Create student led conferences with teachers and parents (teachers).	
		3d. Create homework hotline (SIT, teachers).	

*Included with permission of Thomas Barlow

CONCLUSION

"Entirely too many programs for the development of sound and constructive school-community relations are sporadic in nature, improperly conceived, poorly planned, and crudely executed. They defeat their own purpose. If a school . . . wishes to engage in a comprehensive and continuing program of school-community relations, then it must be willing to plan how its character, needs, and services may be interpreted best to the [parents], how their wishes and aspirations may be interpreted best to the school, and how [parental] involvement may be included in the task of educational improvement and institutional adjustment to social change" (Moore et al. 2016, p. 14).

REFERENCES

Gordon, Ira. (1979). The effects of parent involvement on schooling. In R. S. Brandt (Ed.), *Partners: Parents and schools*. Alexandria, VA: Association for Supervision and Curriculum Development.

Gutman, L. M., & Midgley, C. (2000). The role of protective factors in supporting the academic achievement of poor African American students during the middle school transition. *Journal of Youth and Adolescence, 29*(2), 223–248.

Henderson, A. T., & Berla, N. (1994). *A new generation of evidence: The family is critical to student achievement.* Washington, DC: National Committee for Citizens in Education.

Henderson, A. T., & Mapp, K. L. (2002). A new wave of evidence: The impact of school, family, and community connections on student achievement. Austin, TX: Southwest Educational Development Laboratory.

Kellaghan, T., Sloane, K., Alvarez, B., & Bloom, B. S. (1993). *The home environment & school learning: Promoting parental involvement in the education of children.* San Francisco, CA: Jossey-Bass, Inc.

Lezotte, L. W. (1999). *Correlates of effective schools: The first and second generation.* Okemos, MI: Effective Schools Product, Ltd.

Moore, E. H., Bagin, D. F., & Gallagher, D. R. (2016). *The school and community relations.* Boston, MA: Pearson.

Olsen, G., & Fuller, M. L. (2008). *Home-school relations: Working successfully with parents.* Boston, MA: Pearson.

Olsen, G., & Fuller, M. L. (2010, July 10). *The benefits of parent involvement: What research has to say.* Retrieved May 10, 2016, from http://www.education.com/reference/article/benefits-parent-involvement-research/

Chapter 8

Persistence and Drive—Never Give Up!

> We can, whenever and wherever we choose, successfully teach all children whose schooling is of interest to us. We already know more than we need to do that. Whether or not we do it must finally depend on how we feel about the fact that we haven't so far.—Ronald Edmonds

Few would deny that providing school leadership is increasing in its complexity yearly, if not monthly or weekly. This is an understatement for leaders of urban schools where we find a large number of minority and underserved students, and leaders must tackle the achievement gap often associated with minority and underserved students. Besides the societal issues, leaders are required to address the resistance that comes from teachers, parents/guardians, and students who are reluctant to change or who refuse to change with a mind-set of "this too will pass."

Needless to say, establishing a school climate where every student is expected to learn and the faculty is fully committed to supporting students in the quest is often not an easy task. While mostly every school has some early adopters, those that not only welcome but also embrace change, as educational leaders we inherit or have cultivated a culture that is often lopsided with more school stakeholders who shun change or who draw a line in the sand and refuse to change. They must be overtly convinced of the need to change or through "power plays" be forced to change. Thus, the process is most frequently overly time-consuming and demanding. Regardless, today the pressure is on the educational leader to bring about change, to convert failing and marginal schools into schools of academic excellence.

In spite of the degree of resistance, effective school leaders must be persistent and have the drive to ensure that their schools are academically successful. Effective leaders analyze and look for causes for poor performance and never offer excuses. For effective leaders, excuses are inexcusable. They work tirelessly and unrelentingly, holding themselves accountable and motivating others to achieve. Effective leaders are persistent, resourceful, and creative and demonstrate remarkable drive. Driven by a sound and meaningful vision, if a path is blocked, they find another way. They are like streams of water, meandering, but tenaciously finding a way. They never give up!

UNION NEGOTIATIONS

Educational leaders, especially at the building level, view unions and union agreements differently from school board members. In areas where unions are strong, some building leaders bristle at the mention of unions. They see unions as an impediment to progress. However, teacher unions, besides playing a key role in collective bargaining, offer several benefits. They have been instrumental in improving the learning environment. They have been a voice for teachers in a political system that would, if it could, ignore them. Among other things they have advocated for adequate funding for education, decreased class sizes, professional development opportunities, and other educational reforms. Teacher unions also offer a wide array of professional development opportunities to its members, empowering teachers to do a better job of teaching.

Additionally, teacher unions have been necessary as protection from authoritative, dictatorial, "powercrazed" leaders who arbitrarily administer power. They are a part of a check and balance process. Critics, however, argue that teacher unions have stifled school reform and have moved steadily to control public education by impeding important changes that would make schools more flexible and responsive. They are often blamed for the lack of academic progress. Johnson and Kardos (2000) state that critics regard unions as too powerful, gobbling up the prerogatives of management, and regard contracts as being too constraining. Critics conclude that the role of unions in collective bargaining should be reduced or eliminated.

Advocates of unions, on the other hand, believe that the unions' role in school reform should be enhanced and carefully maintained, especially in the current climate of school reform where among corporate-style reformers the answer to fixing schools today is to put in place autocratic leaders who rule with a whip in hand and an iron fist. They contend that unions can advance and have advanced the cause of school reform. According to Johnson and Kardos (2000), the contract in a local district can provide the framework for improvement, and teachers, along with management, should guide change.

Therefore, advocates conclude that the role of unions in collective bargaining should be maintained and expanded.

Objectively few would contest the point that unions have played a significant role in America and are needed today for fair and impartial treatment of employees. Additionally, there are school districts in which the union has advanced the cause of school reform (Johnson & Kardos, 2000). Experience with union board agreements, however, has convinced some practitioners (Kowalski, 1982) that school boards too often "give away the baby with the bath water." Kowalski refers to administrators who agree too quickly to demands in order to avoid conflict or who refuse to negotiate at all.

Unions should assure fairness and due process but never protect incompetent people who have no desire to improve. Roe (2006) states that instead of unions taking aggressive action to weed out low-performing teachers, unions often protect them and do everything they can to ensure that no one ever loses a job. He adds, "Unions use their power in collective bargaining to pursue teacher (and union) interests that are not the same as the interests of children" (p. 21). School boards should not negotiate and agree to contracts that perpetuate mediocrity. However, as indicated in the Interstate Leadership Licensure Consortium (ISLLC) Standard 5, educational leaders, once a contract has been signed, have an ethical responsibility to respect and abide by the said contract. They also must provide leadership (the ability to influence others) to bring about constructive changes within the confines of the agreement and if necessary take the leadership in eliminating factors that impede the quest for academic excellence.

School officials for many years viewed conflict, according to Hanson (1996), as an undesirable element of organizational life; they went to great lengths to avoid it or to eradicate it quickly. It did not matter what the issue was (paid holidays, use of equipment, amount of homework, access to teacher lesson plans, frequency of teacher observations, grading policies, etc.), the mode of operation was avoidance or submission. Both actions may have saved time and energy, but they actually are nonmanagement choices that almost always produce unforeseen problems. Districts that ratify strong, binding, inflexible union agreements often create roadblocks for the change process.

The strength of unions appears to be diminishing across the nation. Superfine and Gottlieb (2014) note that twenty-four states have in place "right-to-work" provisions under a state constitution or statute. "In a right-to-work state, labor unions and employees may not require employees to join unions or pay union dues as a condition of employment. As such, the power of unions to form and bargain collectively is significantly weakened in these states" (p. 768).

While a trend seems to be developing, in thirty states, if requested by teachers' unions, school districts are required to engage in collective bargaining. "In these states, bargaining can occur over a potentially wide range of issues, including teacher salaries, healthcare, grievance and dismissal procedures, length of the school day and year, and transfer and layoff procedures. Moreover, bargaining may occur over issues that border those that are sometimes left to administrators, such as class size, professional development, coaching, and student discipline" (Superfine & Gottlieb, p. 769). "Collective bargaining is often accused of preventing the assignment of highly effective teachers to struggling schools and increasing the disparities between schools that serve high-minority or high-poverty communities and schools that do not serve predominantly minority or low-income communities. This is largely because many collective bargaining agreements contain strict provisions regarding transfers and vacancy, in which more veteran teachers are given preference in school assignments" (Superfine & Gottlieb, p. 781).

Conditions in employees' contracts may set what may seem as insurmountable barriers on building leadership; however, effective educational leaders do not use the contract as an excuse in their quest of academic excellence. They are resourceful, creative, and persistent in implementing alternatives while respecting and abiding by the conditions of an employees' agreement.

School district leaders should consult with building-level leaders about problematic language and provisions in contractual agreements; however, once ratified, a contract is what it is and should be respected and the provisions abided by. But, effective leaders find ways to respect and abide by a contract and still do what is necessary to effectively manage a school and do what is necessary instructionally. Consider the following:

Possible Problematic Language	*Possible Alternative*
Only one staff meeting per month	Hold grade-level meetings, department meetings or small group meetings as often as is warranted
Duty-free lunch hour	Offer an additional hour pay if a teacher is needed
Seniority rule and incompetent teachers	More frequent teacher observations
Specified minutes for teacher prep	If needed for other task, compensate or offer an extended lunch hour or early departure
Specified class size	Provide a classroom aide or compensation

In the final analysis, according to Roe (2006) the purpose of the public school system is to educate children and to educate them well. Effective educational leaders respect contractual agreements without sacrificing academic excellence. Effective educational leaders find a legal way to get the job done.

UNDERSTANDING RESISTANCE TO CHANGE

If we reflect on the many times that we are responsible for change efforts, often we felt the uneasiness that is associated with change. While some under our supervision by nature are early adopters, most are not. Unless we were the initiators of the change ourselves, we responded to the change effort in various degrees of receptivity. Even if we saw the need for a change, we may have been reluctant to put forth the necessary effort to bring about the change needed or desired. Further reflection would cause us to agree that the change effort evoked a variety of emotions—insecurity, fear, doubt, confusion, and anguish, among others—which were not addressed. Educational leaders are pivotal in the change process, and their success is not automatic or inevitable.

There are many factors that can influence and affect the success of school improvement efforts. Success is less likely to occur without the leader and the school improvement committee developing an understanding of and demonstrating the technical skills necessary to introduce and implement the desired change. Educational leaders and others who have tried to implement change are fully aware of the complexity of the change process; however, those of us who have experienced any significant degree of success were effective in dealing with resistance.

ANTICIPATE AREAS OF RESISTANCE

Adenle (2011) says most people typically avoid situations that upset the order of things and prefer predictability and stability in both their personal and professional lives. Evans (1996) points out that "most attempts at collective change in education seem to fail, and failure means frustration, wasted time, feelings of incompetence and lack of support, and disillusion" (p. 73). A repeated failure with attempts to change establishes a climate that drastically reduces a school's impetus and capacity to change. Given the present demand for change and the need for schools to change if they are to meet the needs of its clients, the students, it is highly recommended that we anticipate where we might meet resistance.

While there is abundance of research on the topic why people resist change (Adenle, 2011; Rick, 2011; Tanner, 2015), based on many years of experience in public education and at the collegiate level, the following reasons are offered:

- **Confusion about the need for change/reason is unclear**—Often with poor communication the faculty and staff, especially those who feel the current way is working, do not understand the need for change.
- **Incompetence**—People in general do not like to admit to being incompetent. Changes in operations of and delivery of instruction often demand skill changes and leave the faculty and staff feeling that they may not be able to make the necessary transitions. The question becomes: given the requirements associated with the change, will I be able to fulfill my responsibilities successfully? If the answer is no, there is a chance of resistance.
- **Anxiety associated with the unknown**—Most people are not risk takers. They feel safe with the status quo and tend to cling to the past because it is more secure. They become fearful when they know little about the impact of the change. The less they know about a change, the more fearful they are. Questionable surprises create fear. Anxiety is a result of fear and is a strong emotion. It is such a strong emotion that when change is presented that has not been presented properly, the emotion manifests itself in the form of resistance.
- **Invested in old behaviors**—There is comfort and assurance in doing things the old way, especially if the old way is perceived by stakeholders as working. Faculty and staff often are emotionally tied to the present way of doing things.
- **Little or no trust**—In organizations or schools where mistrust exists and stakeholders do not feel they are supported, they tend to resist change. Meaningful change does not occur in a climate of mistrust. When leaders have not created a climate for change, that is, they have not been fair ethical and demonstrated the competency to lead the change process, there is plenty room for resistance on the part of faculty and staff. Trust involves people having faith in others' intentions.
- **Oversaturation**—When every year or two another change is mandated, faculty and staff begin to think that changes are being made for change sake. The change process overwhelms them. The end result is low motivation; the faculty and staff do not commit themselves to the change. They resist the change, and if the change is imposed, they play the waiting game until the next change is presented.
- **Poor communication**—In any organization or school, the way the change is communicated is critical in determining its level of acceptance. Changes that are imposed with little communication or through poor methods are often poorly received. Good communication gives people more assurance. There is never too much communication.

- **A mind-set of "this too shall pass"**—Often faculty and staff believe that the change initiative is a temporary fad. Since they see it as a fad, they fail to commit to the change.
- **Changes to routines**—Routines allow faculty and staff to operate in their comfort zones. People like predictability and stability. Doing things differently brings about insecurity and resistance.
- **Limited or no input**—People want to know what is going on and have an opportunity for input. They customarily do not like the wills of others imposed on them. If they are not allowed to be a part of the change, and have little or no input, resistance may occur.
- **Personal benefits and rewards**—For many faculty and staff the organization or school does not come first; they come first. They will resist change when they do not see any rewards for themselves forthcoming from the change. The question becomes "what is in it for me? Are the benefits and rewards for making the change adequate for the trouble involved?" If the answer is nothing or no, the response may present itself in the form of resistance. Without some reward, they see no reason or motivation to support the change.
- **Potential of job loss**—People are reluctant to make changes that are viewed as harmful to their current situation. Faculty and staff may resist changes that may result in their role in the school being eliminated or reduced.
- **Loss of control**—Familiar routines tend to give people a sense of control over their work responsibilities. Change may make people feel powerless and bewildered.
- **Improper timing**—Timing is important. Changes imposed or mandated at the wrong time may lead to resistance. When the conditions have not been properly established for change, change is more difficult. Organizations and schools need to prepare for change.
- **Internal politics**—Every organization or school has internal politics present within. If the change is not viewed positively, internal politics may be used to prevent the change. Organizations also have power wielders who may or may not be liked or trusted. If they are not liked or trusted, resistance may present itself.
- **Demise of support system**—People like knowing that they have leaders and other colleagues that will support them in challenging times. Changing the organizational structure may lead to fear and resistance.
- **Previous negative experience**—Our past experiences color our perspective of the present and the future. People who have had negative experiences as a result of a change are likely to fear change and resist changes.
- **Fellow sympathy**—Stakeholders often resist change to protect coworkers, colleagues, and friends on the job. Social attachment is a part of life and is a strong emotion.

- **Disregard of influential**—All organizations and schools have power wielders, people who influence others. When leaders introduce change without winning over and convincing those who influence others to buy in to the change, there can be resistance.
- **Wrong leadership**—Sometimes the problem is not the change, but who is providing the leadership. Sometimes the leader is not liked or disrespected, and this may lead to resistance. Other times it is not the change, but how the leader implements the change process. Interpersonal skills make a difference. People make organization succeed and people make organizations fail.

In summary, most people prefer predictability and stability in all phases of their lives. Typically, they avoid situations that threaten order in their lives, increase stress in their lives, eliminate the comfort zones in their lives, and involve nerve-racking risks. When faced with changes to the status quo, except the small percentage of those labeled risk-takers, people generally resist initially. Expecting resistance to change and planning for it will prepare you to manage the course of action. Being aware of and understanding the most common reasons why people resist change allows you to be prepared to overcome the resistance.

Resistance is not just expressed verbally; often resistance is also exhibited in negative behavior. Being cognizant of negative behavior indicators will allow you to build a line of defense. Just as a football coach leads team members in studying the opposing team, educational leaders should lead a school improvement team in studying areas of resistance, the enemies of change. Adenle (2011) notes that it is better to anticipate areas of resistance and address them in your management plan than to spend your time putting out fires when that time could be better used implementing the change.

DEALING WITH DIFFICULT TEACHERS

Any building leader who claims that he loves dealing with difficult teachers would be in most opinions labeled as insane. The truth is no one looks forward to it, even if you think you are "mighty than Thou." However, it does not mean that we cannot work to prevent unproductive behavior that leads to conflict. Almost all schools have at least one teacher who works against school improvements and who does not have the best interest of students in mind.

Difficult behavior manifests itself in many ways. It includes gossiping, ignoring other stakeholders, yelling, harassing others, ignoring directives, being rude, shutting down, complaining to your superiors—the list goes on and on. Difficult behavior is often a result of psychological needs for control, recognition, affection, and respect. Difficult teachers "work" the principal; documentation, investigations, and hearings are all time-consuming. They cause time to be used that should be consumed in other meaningful ways in the quest for academic excellence.

When educational leaders can successfully lead a difficult staff member to change negative behavior, they increase their credibility with the rest of the staff. It should not be surprising that good teachers want principals to deal with challenging teachers. Unhappy people make others unhappy and not just the principal. Additionally, good teachers are embarrassed, ashamed, and humiliated by the negative behavior of difficult colleagues. They recognize that negative behavior discolors the image of the entire school. If educational leaders fail to address the behavior of difficult teachers, they will allow these teachers to poison the school's climate and culture. A teacher who resists change covertly or who is just plain hard to work with can inject negativity into the school's climate and culture. A few such teachers can derail change (Eller & Eller, 2013).

Although it is easy to label people as difficult, the real focus should always be on the actual behavior. One may not be able to change the personalities of difficult teachers, but you can change their behavior. "Effective leaders must find ways to motivate their employees to provide maximum success for the organization. In today's world of high accountability, this ability is paramount to the success and survival of our schools, and is an especially important skill for early career principals to master" (Eller & Eller, 2012b, p. 29).

Eller and Eller (2012a) identify the characteristics of eight types of difficult and resistant colleagues and offer strategies to deal with each. The first is the "Underminers" who they note will say that they will comply, but behind your back will criticize and fail to implement. Stressing that it is important to give everyone a fair chance, they suggest that you visit their classrooms to check on implementation. Noncompliance should be confronted in private sessions. They identify a group called the "Contrarians" who ignore others' perspectives and believe that if they don't speak up, they will be perceived as totally agreeable, compromising their own position. In dealing with the "Contrarians," they suggest that you plan pro-and-con discussions with all staff requesting new ideas and strategies and require that all suggestion have a focus on teaching and learning.

Then, Eller and Eller identify the "Recruiters" who exude concerted effort to draw others, especially those who are new or unsure, into accepting their point of view and in doing so often drop names of those who support their view. In response to this group, they suggest that you empower others to speak for themselves and that you challenge "Recruiters" to verify those who supposedly agree with them; use difficult conversation to confront this behavior. Next, are the "Challenged" who do not believe change is necessary because they are doing a good job. They often mask their lack of knowledge. In responding to the "Challenged," it is advised that you ask them specific questions to see if they understand what is being proposed. If there are gaps and deficiencies noted, provide information via coaching, peer modeling, and conferencing.

Another interesting group is the "Retired on the job." These persons reveal in their behavior and sometimes words that they are not motivated to change or improve. They prefer to be left alone until they are eligible for retirement. In countering this group, it is suggested that you state your expectations about the work that is required and you follow up with classroom observations. Every school or organization has the "Resident Experts." These are the know-it-alls who proclaim their knowledge about every topic or issue. They refuse to accept responsibility for their errors, often blaming others. They make excuses when you want to observe them demonstrating their skills and expertise. It is suggested by Eller and Eller that you privately question them and hold them accountable for their errors. Their behavior is confronted in direct conversation.

Then, there are the "Unelected representatives," who claim to speak for and represent others without their permission. They stir up resistance and negative sentiment toward the change or new initiative. In reaction, ask the staff members they claim to represent them if they truly represent them or not. Additionally, you can conduct open discussion about issues, giving everyone a chance for input. Lastly, Eller and Eller identify the "Whiners and Complainers," who find fault with everything and are quite vocal in talking about their issues and problems. They are persistent in talking about what is not going well for them. They fail to accept personal responsibility. It is suggested that you confront them in conversations, sharing positive ideas and addressing concerns. You should refuse to accept irrational explanations with a focus on reducing the melodrama.

Eller and Eller (2012b) state that directly confronting is one way to deal with negative and difficult staff members. This, they say, can be highly effective because other staff members see that you are concerned and doing something about their issues. Failure to address negative behavior sends a message that the behavior is acceptable. They add that the educational leader should work to develop the strengths of the other staff members to minimize the development or impact of the difficult and resistant staff. They offer two strategies they found helpful in building the strength of a school's employee. The first is that you conduct individual meetings with staff to discuss their perceptions of and ideas and aspiration for the school. In these meetings specific questions are asked about the positive aspects of the school, recommendations for changes or adjustments are sought, and ideas and strategies to effectively implement new ideas are requested. The second suggestion is that you hold "difficult conversations" with difficult staff. They suggest that the tone of the meeting should be serious and that you provide specific examples of the problem, tell the person what is expected, make sure the directives are understood, and the steps that will be taken to make sure the expectations are fulfilled. Eller and Eller conclude that even though a minority of your staff may be considered to be difficult, their influence can be major if not addressed (Eller & Eller, 2012b). "A hint to the wise should be sufficient!"

Orloff (2014) in her book, *The Ecstasy of Surrender*, describes five difficult workplace types and some communication strategies for each type. She identifies the "Narcissist" who can be obnoxious or quite charming, but has an inflated sense of importance and entitlement, and craves attention. She warns us to not fool ourselves into believing we can gain their loyalty and love. To get our goals met with the "Narcissist," she urges us to stoke their egos and frame our request in ways that are meaningful to them, showing them how our request will be beneficial to them.

The "Passive-Aggressive Coworker" is next. This type expresses anger while smiling or showing excessive concern. With sometimes clenched teeth, they remain calm and collected. This type should be spoken to directly and their behavior specifically addressed. Let them know their behavior is hurtful. Remember, people do to you what you give them permission to do. Then, there is the "Gossip." These are those who experience joy talking about others behind their backs, spreading damaging rumors, and expressing "put-downs." Their behavior is often toxic. In dealing with the "Gossip' type, Orloff recommends you confront them letting them know that their comments are inconsiderate and hurtful to others. Attempt to get them to see how they would feel if they were the recipient of such negativity. Lastly, avoid sharing personal information with them and attempt to ignore them.

The "Anger Addict" has a raging personality and handles conflict by accusing, attacking, humiliating, or criticizing, according to Orloff. It is suggested that you gain control of yourself first, pausing before you speak. To defuse them, recognize their position, but share your position in a polite manner; you have a right to differ. Empathize and seek compromise, regardless how small. Seeking and understanding the reasons why the "Anger Addict" behaves the way they do may lead to other strategies and approaches. Finally, Orloff identifies the "Guilt Tripper." This type is the blamers, the sacrificial lambs, and the drama kings and queens. They know how to pull the emotional strings to your heart, making you feel insecure and terrible. Orloff recommends the following strategies in dealing with the type: point out that everyone makes mistakes and you are not perfect, apologize if you feel one is warranted, and let them know that you are human and have feelings too, and it hurts when they say things the way that they do.

In *Dealing with People You Can't Stand*, Brinkman and Kirschner (2011) identify ten classic problem types and offer strategies to address each. Based on twenty years of personal experience, they have identified and outlined six of them that are thought to be most destructive :

"**TANK**"- Is confrontational • Wants to control the process and get things done • Exhibits behavior that ranges from pushiness to outright aggression • STRATEGIES: Command respect • Hold your ground • Establish peace with honor, expressing the need for all to get along together.

"**SNIPER**"—Attempts to control you through embarrassment and humiliation• Uses rude comments, sarcasm and rolling of the eyes. STRATEGIES: Bring the sniper out of hiding • Question their behavior and statements • Make the "Sniper" uncomfortable.

"**GRENADES**"—Feels unappreciated and disrespected and explodes •Rants and raves.

STRATEGIES: Take control of the situation • Get their attention • Be positive that your tone and language are friendly • Show genuine, sincere concern • Strive to reduce the intensity of the conflict.

"**KNOW-IT-ALL**"—Is knowledgeable and competent • Intends to get it done in the way they have predetermined are best • Needs attention • Fools the people some of time but not all of the time • Does not accept responsibility for errors.

STRATEGIES: Open them up to new ideas • Be prepared and know your stuff • Present your views respectfully • Recognize their expertise • Provide them respectful mentors.

"**THINK-THEY-KNOW-IT-ALL**"—Is a specialist in exaggeration, half-truths, jargon, useless advice, and unsolicited opinions • Is charismatic and desperate for attention.

STRATEGIES: Find an acceptable way to disavow their unworkable ideas • Provide them a little attention • Get clarification for specifics • Be patient • Gently confront them with the consequences of their negative behavior • Credit the things they do right.

"**NO**"—Kills momentum and creates friction • Finds the negatives in everyone and everything.

STRATEGIES: Attempt to move them from fault finding to problem solving • Use them as a resource • Do not push for an immediate decision • Acknowledge their good intent.

This author had experiences during his twenty years as a building principal with all of these. In one school, he had a daughter of one of the central administrators of the district. She was a combination of a Sniper and a Know-It-All type. Obviously her contacts kept her well informed. She would attempt to upstage me at faculty meetings, sharing sometimes information that had not been shared with the author. In dealing with her, he allowed her to be the source of knowledge if it was in line with the agenda; however, he always researched her topics and made it his business to become as knowledgeable as she and would revisit the matter at future meetings showing his knowledge base and often correcting her errors. At that same school, this author had a "No" teacher. She found fault with everything most colleagues suggested. In listening to her, he concluded that she could be a resource; he convinced her to conduct workshops. He discovered that when she was given some attention and responsibilities, she was less negative and more respective of others.

In Armstrong's (2011a,b) work, *4 Strategies Help Educators Overcome Resistance to Change*, he identifies three common types of resistance encountered by professionals. The first is *Aggressive resistance* and is the easiest type to identify because it is overt and there is no effort to disguise it. Aggressive behavior types tend to be hostile, verbally or physically abusive, sarcastic, opinioned, and selfish. You are inclined to hear these people say, "I don't care what the principal says, I will not participate."

The second kind identified is *Passive-Aggressive resistance*, which can be called "sugarcoated hostility." It is the indirect expression of hostility. It is manifested through behavior, such as procrastination, stubbornness, or deliberate or repeated failure to accomplish requested tasks. Colleagues of this type appear willing to change or support, but the change and the support never materialize. You are likely to hear these staff members say, "I am willing to assist, but I need to finish doing my other work." The other work never is completed. Instead you get excuses.

Lastly, Armstrong points to a difficult form of resistance, *Passive resistance*. Staff members who are passive in nature often may be dishonest and often avoid situations or solving problems hoping they will get resolved on their own. They exhibit a "whatever" attitude. They complain to others instead of the person who needs to hear the complaint. They appear to be wholeheartedly acceptable, until action fails to take place. They seem enthusiastic, but they never follow through. You hear them say, "Excellent idea, let's do it." You never see any results, any action.

McEwan (2005) in *How to Deal with Teachers Who Are Angry, Troubled, Exhausted, or Just Plain Confused* outlines how to deal with difficult teachers. Whether your goal is to take the lead in reforming a dysfunctional school or to deal with one or two difficult teachers, She suggests an effective leader should put seven habits of attitude and action into daily practice, namely, *being an assertive administrator* who is not distracted from the school' mission by teachers' inappropriate behaviors; *being a character builder*, a role model whose values, words, and deeds are marked by trustworthiness, integrity, competency, ethicalness, and humility—one who becomes the picture you are painting, the sermon you are preaching, and the change you want to see; *being a communicator*, "a genuine and open human being with the capacity to listen, empathize, interact, and connect with teachers in productive, helping, and healing ways" (p. 10); *nurturing a positive school culture* paying scrupulous attention to your deeds and words, everything you do and say; *being a contributor*, demonstrating servant leadership; *conducting assertive interventions*, helping every teacher to become aware of and to overcome negative behaviors that stand in the way of their productivity in the classroom and the achievement of the school's vision; and *doing it today*—not procrastinating, looking for the proper time; the ideal time is today.

McEwan concludes that each of these habits is essential to dealing with difficult teachers and, if practiced daily, will strengthen and enhance your instructional leadership. She adds, however, if you are unwilling to confront incompetence or a lack of commitment to the school's mission among even a few faculty members, you will pay the price in the following ways:

- Lowered teacher morale
- The devaluation of the school's effective teachers
- Loss of trust and respect from parents and students—for you individually as well as your school
- Loss of teacher efficacy and empowerment
- A downward spiral of academic achievement and an upward spiral of behavioral problems (McEwan, 2005)

It should be noted that in her works, McEwan (2005) states that while she has focused on certified staff, her recommendations and strategies are applicable to all staff members. An angry custodian, a disgruntled instructional aide, or a mean cafeteria worker can impact the culture of a school just as an angry, troubled, exhausted, or just plain confused teacher.

In closing, consider the following in dealing with difficult staff:

- **Don't Take It Personally**—Difficult persons behave inappropriately with many persons. Try to stay focused on the negative behavior you want to improve or eliminate.
- **Control Self**—When you lose control, the situation probably will get worse.
- **Analyze the Incident**—Determine if it is the person or a difficult situation. Try to get to the root of the problem. If it is the situation, you may want to have an open discussion of the matter.
- **Consider the Impact**—Do you address the behavior or ignore it? If the negative behavior is not major or repetitive, it might be best left alone.
- **Focus on the Behavior and Not the Person**—You can't always lead a person to change, but you can change or control behavior.

- **Listen to Others**—Even though you disagree, allow colleagues who demonstrate difficult behavior to verbally express themselves. Doing so will give you insights.
- **Inform**—Often difficult persons know that they are being difficult and are rewarded by being difficult. However, there are times when colleagues are unaware of their impact on others—a blind self. A first step toward resolving conflict is to engage the person in a conversation about unproductive behavior.
- **Reality Check**—Recognize that difficult issues don't disappear. Sweeping matters under the rug will eventually cause stumbling blocks! Compressing things often causes an explosion! Don't procrastinate!

DEALING WITH UNRULY PARENTS

As an educational leader, you probably were in position only a few days before you had the misfortune of dealing with a difficult parent or family or had a conflict with a parent. Here are some strategies, tried and tested, that may help to alleviate many, if not all, of the problems with parents:

- **Remember who is the professional**—We are! We have had training; during conflicts is the time to use it. We cannot exhibit the same behavior of unruly parents. More fuel on the fire only leads to great combustion. Someone has to be in control of self. While we would hope all parties involved will be in control of self, if no one else is, the professional should be.

I have had situations where parents have threatened to "kick my butt." I have respectfully and assertively advised them that the school corporation doesn't pay me enough to take "butt beatings," and I have assured them that I was not going to stand there and take it, but I was sure as adults we could work it out. If the threats continued, I removed myself from the situation and called security. When necessary, charges were filed with the prosecutor to let parents know that negative behavior would not be tolerated in the school.

I cannot count the times I have been cursed by parents. Without a doubt being raised in an urban community, I learned to curse. However, as a professional I consistently during my six years as a teacher and twenty years as a principal resisted the temptation of allowing unruly parents to cause me to curse them. I would ask two or three times for the parent to calm down. If they failed to do so, I would walk out of my office and leave them there. I welcomed them back when they came in a peaceful manner. My parents learned what I expected of them.

- **Build trust and confidence**—Once you have conflict with a parent, put that parent on radar. Do your homework communicating often with the parent, advising him or her of the progress of the child. Work to connect with the parent. Do this so effectively that when the child complains about you, the parent will conclude that what is reported, especially if it is false or distorted, does not sound like you. Work to earn parents' respect. It works!
- **Have an open-door policy**—Let parents know that you are available to discuss their concerns. Allow parents to call you at home. Try to avoid letting the sun to go down on their wrath allowing anger to simmer all night.
- **Set limits to unruly behavior**—As indicated earlier, parents need to know that behavior that negatively disturbs the school's climate will not be tolerated.

During an awards ceremony, a parent was upset because his daughter did not receive a perfect attendance award. In the midst of the program, he came up on the stage and loudly confronted me. I advised him of the guidelines for the award. He disagreed with the guidelines and boisterously advised me that he would "kick my a_ _." In an effort to restore some decorum to the ceremony, I got up and left the auditorium. He followed me to the office, cursing me all the way there. Once we got to the office, the head secretary who had some rapport with him convinced him to leave. I did not let the matter go. I filed charges with the county prosecutor. Later I dropped the charges, but I had established with the parent that I would not tolerate such behavior.

In another incident, a parent was upset about her son being punished by a teacher for using foul language. The parent was known for fighting in the community. Many teachers were afraid of this parent, her siblings, and her mother. I tried to reason with the parent, but the parent was determined to beat me and the teacher. After a while she was convinced to leave the school grounds. I did not let the matter drop. I sent her a certified letter indicating that such behavior would not be tolerated and that if she came to the school ground again behaving in a like manner, she would be banned from the school grounds and all school activities. Weeks later I saw her at the bank, and she approached me apologizing. Remember, this was a parent who had embedded fear in most, if not all, of the staff.

- **Don't make knee-jerk decisions**—If an angry parent contacts you and you have time before a meeting, try to ascertain the concern; then do your homework, seeking as much information as you can about the matter. If a teacher or other staff member is the subject of the complaint, confer with him or her. Talk with other teachers and staff who work with the student. Be prepared as possible, and avoid letting the goals of the meeting be just those of the parent. The parent may want to vent, but your goal should be child centered; if so, you can offer a clear plan of action. If you do not have time to prepare for the meeting, do not make a decision before speaking with the all involved stakeholders.

- **Prevent surprise attacks**—If the parent is not angry with you, but with another staff member, avoid bringing that person into a meeting initially. Give the parent an opportunity to calm down. After allowing the parent to vent, suggest a time for a meeting with all involved, at a later date. This will give the parent additional time to cool off. If a meeting must occur immediately, never bring colleagues into the meeting without informing them of the nature of the meeting.
- **Start on a positive note**—Set the tone of meetings. Focus on the child. Assure the parent "we are all here with the interest of your child in mind and to do what is best for your child."
- **Be an active listener**—You must listen with three ears for what the parent is saying, what the parent is not saying, and what the parent is trying to say. Try not to show nonverbal behavior such as facial expressions and gestures that may further irritate the parent. Keep a relaxed posture and use eye contact. Try to identify with the parents' concerns recognizing that love blinds and protects persons. While venting some parents can be long-winded and repetitive, but avoid interrupting. However, you should ask relevant questions and clarify. Summarize the main points, feelings, and concerns expressed.
- **Don't show the child disunion**—If possible, don't bring the student in until you and the parent are at least somewhat on the same side or with the same mind-set. It is better to attempt to work things out before the child is in the room. If you need to seek information from the child during the investigation stage, attempt to confer with the child in a separate setting. Children need to see the school and the parent are on the same page.
- **Agree on specific steps**—Pick two or three practical steps each of you can take. If you are going to find something out for the parent, tell them you'll get back to them and do so.
- **Support consistently with follow-through**—On the part of the school assure the parent that you will implement and monitor agreed-upon resolutions. Then do it. Schedule a follow-up meeting. Do not wait a month or a semester for another conflict to occur. Doing these things will build credibility, develop stability, and create school support.
- **Be a vision-builder**—Before the conclusion of a conflict resolution meeting, use the time with affected stakeholders as a chance to communicate the vision and mission of the school.

Besides dealing with unruly and difficult parents, the school leader has the task of engaging and motivating parents to join the vision team. Effective school leaders not only focus attention on every aspect of the school's vision but also communicate the vision clearly and convincingly. They create opportunities for interchange with multiple stakeholders through participatory communication strategies. They attend to aspects of the school as an organization and a community, with consideration of external relationships (Leithwood & Riehl, 2003). They understand that if a school is to move forward, there must be an engagement of all stakeholders in realizing the vision. As they inspire others to reach the school's goals, they understand that parents are key; thus, engagement must focus on parents. After all, we get more touchdowns when all the team members are working together.

There is growing evidence that family and community connections with schools make a difference in student success. When schools and families work together, research shows that children tend to do better in school, stay in school longer, and like school more (Henderson & Mapp, 2002). While there are numerous ways to engage parents and motivate them to become full partners in the quest of academic excellence, the following suggestions are offered:

- **Communicate frequently with parents using all means of external communication.** Share with them the vision, the goals, and the achievements of the school. Even try streamlining PTA and PTSO meetings and workshops.
- **Build relationships.** Practice contacting parents before there are problems. Focus on the positive. Share school experiences so parents feel informed. Develop the habit of calling, texting, or e-mailing two or three parents each night.
- **Involve yourself in the community.** Let parents and others know how much you care. Parents don't care what you know until they know how much you care. Join them in the high and low points of their lives and those of their children. In other words, attend funerals, visit the sick, drop in during a birthday party, make a call, and so on. If you show concern for your students and their parents, then they'll be more willing to work with you throughout the school year.
- **Empower parents to be able to assist their children with homework and class assignments.** Conduct parent workshops on state standards, academic areas of weakness, the school improvement plan, math skills, reading skills, and so on.
- **Entice parents/guardians into the school.** Schedule Parent Science Fairs, Friday Read-a-thons, Math Fairs, Scholarly Game Nights, Breakfast with Grandparents, and other such academic enrichment activities. Such activities will engage parents and allow you to give them ideas of how to support the academic program with family fun activities.

- **For school breaks print and distribute bulletins with fun activities that support the academic program and reduce regression.**
- **Make home visits**. Today many educational leaders shy away from making home visits, but they work. If everything else fails, the best approach might be to offer parents the option of meeting with them in their home. Not only will most parents appreciate the effort, but many times, you will learn something about the lives of your students and their families.

Research clearly shows that there is a strong positive relationship between student success in school and the level of engagement of parents with the school (Henderson & Mapp, 2002; Van Voorhis, 2001). Most practitioners will admit that one of the biggest challenges they face is that of engaging parents or other guardians meaningfully and consistently in their children's academic pursuits. Needless to say, all effective educational leaders not only desire but also strive to get parents to become more involved in their children's education.

CONVERTING UNWILLING STUDENTS

All school personnel must deal with students who engage in behaviors that are disruptive to the educational process. These behaviors range from less disruptive behaviors such as students being late for class, leaving early, sleeping in class, acting as the class clown or talking inappropriately to more offensive behavior such as bullying, cyber bulling, stalking, fighting, using drugs, cursing, and being physically or verbally disrespectful to teachers and other adults. If ignored or improperly handled, one single disruptive act can have a long-term impact on classroom atmosphere. Misbehavior left unchecked may escalate to intolerable or dangerous levels.

Few, if any, school leaders desire and seek conflict. Most desire to avoid it. This is the case with student conflict. While you may have to address disruptive student behavior the first day of school, you should work smarter and not harder. This calls for devoting time in preventing, rather than responding to, disruptive behavior. Following are suggested ways to prevent and reduce negative behavior in the school:

- Identify at-risk students and provide them intervention programs before problems arise.
- Focus on the affective domain—spend time addressing values and proper behavior.
- Get to know students—each is unique—and show them that you care.
- Work on building rapport with students. Every nut has a hard shell, but if you are successful in cracking the shell outside, you can get the meat inside.

- Build rapport with families of students who demonstrate some early signs of antisocial behavior.
- Involve parents during the school day and at school events.
- Conduct workshops on how to properly solve problems for both students and parents.
- Connect troubled students and their families with social service agencies.
- Work on building school spirit and getting students to like coming to school.
- Give respect to all students and treat them fairly.
- Discipline with love—let students know you dislike the behavior but love them.
- Celebrate the events in student's lives—birthdays, achievements, special events.
- Empower all teachers to be effective classroom managers—conduct focused workshops during the summer and immediately before the start of the school year; intensely monitor during the first few days of the school year; provide opportunities for faculty to share classroom management strategies.
- Have a school-wide and class discipline plan with classroom rules, hall rules, bus rules, lunchroom, and assembly rules.
- Remember that the school day is from the time the students leave home to the time that they return.

Many behavior problems stem from the classroom. Student behavior in classroom may be the single major reason why teachers feel stress in the classroom and leave the teaching profession (Houghton et al., 1988; Van der Doef & Maes, 2002). Poor classroom management, poor classroom climate, and poor teacher planning are usually the causes. Universities, colleges, and other teacher preparatory programs often do not prepare preservice teachers adequately to address student behavior problems; they come in with little or no skills in handling disruptive students (Lannie & McCurdy, 2007; Walker, Ramsey, & Gresham, 2003/2004). If you inherit teachers with weak classroom management skills, you should work to empower them. Here are some suggestions:

- Establish with teachers that you fully expect them to control students and will hold them accountable for student behavior in their classrooms
- Inspire teachers to share with their students often the vision of the school
- Encourage teachers to establish a positive relationship with students—they can be disciplinarians and still have the respect and love of students
- Encourage teachers to engage students in learning from the moment that the bell rings—use "bell ringers" and other warm-up activities.
- Stress with teachers the power of praise and high expectations

- Foster with teachers the need and the importance of sharing the objectives of lessons and why the objectives are important
- Stress with teachers the importance of involving students in instruction
- Encourage teachers to seek ways to liven up instruction and reduce boredom
- Urge teachers to overplan the day leaving no time for distractions. You can stay on task if you plan properly
- Inspire teachers to respect attention span—while you overplan the day, it is important to infuse constructive mental break times into the day. Use meaningful instructional motor activities, humor, and so on
- Discourage teachers from making empty threats—make sure the promised punishment is fair and is done
- Foster in teachers an understanding of the difference between punishment and discipline—punishing is what we do to get students to become disciplined in their behavior
- Inspire teachers to keep in touch with parents—utilize parents in controlling the behavior of students
- Encourage teachers to give the student a "pass" or "break" the first time with low level offenses
- Urge teachers to be in control of their anger and their actions
- Persuade teachers to admit when they are wrong—they are human
- Inspire teachers to attempt to diffuse, rather than infuse a negative situation
- Caution teachers on debating and arguing with students—say what you have to say and attempt to move on

While we work concertedly to prevent negative behavior, it will still occur. When it does, the effective educational leader must know how to address and, hopefully, prevent the reoccurrence.

All students will not exhibit negative or disruptive behavior, but among them will be those who are not producing up to their potential. They have not bought into the vision or may not have been invited to become a vision builder. Keep in mind that the whole is the sum total of its parts. Any student who is not adding to the excellence of a school is subtracting from the school's excellence. What should this mean to the effective school leaders? It means that in addition to preventing and addressing disruptive behavior, the effective school leader must focus on student motivation.

Students, especially those in urban settings, arrive at school with diverse academic skills and behaviors; their needs are great. Unfortunately, these urban school classrooms are staffed with poorly prepared or neophyte teachers with little or no knowledge or experience to address the often-present achievement gap (Lannie & McCurdy, 2007). However, when efforts are made, evidence supports the effectiveness of educational interventions that address the need of underachieving school students (Jackson et al., 2011). The following are some suggestions:

- Review school goals and objectives with students
- Praise student for achievement
- Hold high expectations for students; children tend to fulfill the expectations communicated to them by adults
- Give low-performing students classroom and school responsibilities
- Make learning relevant; work to connect school to the lives and needs of students and connect abstract learning to concrete situations
- Involve students in tracking and monitoring their academic progress
- Expand low-performing student's experiences via trips and excursions
- Reward students for academic achievements
- Provide group student counseling
- Provide individual student counseling
- Provide parent counseling
- Provide tutoring—peer and professional
- Involve low-performing students in the teaching process
- Provide meaningful and constructive feedback on assignments—don't just return papers and other assignments
- Utilize homework hotlines
- Encourage teachers to infuse creativity and life in their lessons
- Encourage teacher to be available to students before and after class and during breaks
- Form teacher-student book clubs
- Create mentoring programs, pairing teachers and other professionals with low-performing students
- Use positive competition in classrooms

While motivating students can be a difficult task, the returns are more than worth it. Motivated students are more excited to learn and participate. Once motivated, teaching becomes less of a task and more enjoyable for teacher and student alike. Many students are self-motivated and have a natural desire to learn. They may learn in spite of the teacher. Good teachers can reach students who do not have this natural drive and inspire them to reach their full potential. It is ultimately the responsibility of the educational leader to stimulate teachers to have the desire to inspire all students and to empower them to be able to do so.

BE THE CHANGE YOU WANT TO SEE

As the shift of accountability moves more and more to the instructional leader, it is clear to me that educational leaders must be the change that they want to see. Change starts and ends with the educational leader, and the educational leader must realize that "change starts and ends with me." He or she must be representative of the sermon that is preached, the picture that is painted, and the song that is sung. Additionally, the educational leader must convert others from me-ism into we-ism. All stakeholders must become a part of the mind-set that if it is to be, it is up to me. Therefore, each individual must come to realize and believe that "change starts and ends with me." It begins with the personal vision for the child, the classroom, and the school, the collective accountability for the success of every child, the commitment to ensure rigor, the willingness to take risks and to support others, and the disdain for failure.

Vision building is the key to overcoming resistance. The most effective and lasting visions are shared ones. When all stakeholders are working together to achieve the vision, when all stakeholders are in quest of academic excellence, positive changes will occur. It is the effective educational leader's responsibility to continually focus and refocus the conversation on the vision and mission of the school. It is so easy for stakeholders to become focused on their personal agendas. Often stakeholders disguise their personal interest with the argument that their interest is in the best interest of the child; however, close analysis and scrutiny will reveal that this is not the case.

Finally, change is successful only if the people being asked to change see the need. While there might be resistance failure occurs when we as educational leaders fail to establish the undying commitment of the people who can impact the change. A collective commitment to improve, combined with a commitment to support the people who take risks and make changes, is necessary.

There must be an expectation that every student will learn and the faculty and staff must be committed to making sure that happens. Key to the realization of this expectation is a strong instructional leader. Failure cannot be an option. Consider these:

Beatitudes for Principals:

Blessed are principals who are willing to make a
difference for theirs is a school of excellence.

Blessed are the principal who serve as change agents
for difficult teachers for they shall be comforted.

Blessed are principals who treat all teachers with dignity
and respect during the change process for they shall
inherit an A+ school.

Blessed are principals who hunger and thirst for excellence,
communicating and shepherding the school's vision
for they shall achieve it and be satisfied.

Blessed are principals who are merciful and fair in
their leadership style, not harassing, threatening, intimidating, or
humiliating for they shall obtain a collegial and collaborative staff.

Blessed are principals who are pure and genuine in
their efforts, guiding and challenging all stakeholder
for they shall see their students achieve.

Blessed are principals who are willing to be the example,
keeping children first, and including and respecting
all stakeholders for they shall be called the
Champions of Leaders, the Role Models Exemplars,
the Principals of A+ Schools.

REFERENCES

Adenle, C. (2011). *Twelve reasons employees resist change in the workplace.* Retrieved July 28, 2015, from http://catherinescareercorner.com/2011/07/26/12-reasonswhyemployeesresist changeintheworkplace/

Armstrong, A. (2011a, Winter). 4 strategies help educators overcome resistance to change. *Tools for Schools, 14*(2), 1–8.

Armstrong, A. (2011b). 4 key strategies help educators overcome resistance to change. *Tools for School, 14*(1), 1–7.

Brinkman, R., & Kirschner, R. (2011). *Dealing with people you can't stand.* NY: McGraw Hill Companies.

Drake, T. L., & Roe, W. H. (1994). *School business management: Supporting instructional effectiveness.* Boston, MA: Allyn and Bacon.

Eller, J. F., & Eller, S. A. (2012a, September/October). Working productively with difficult and resistant staff. *Principal, 92*(1), 28–31. Posted by Michael Keany on October 5, 2012 at 4:44pm in Art of Leadership.

Eller, J. F., & Eller, S. A. (2012b, September/October). Early career principals: Working productively with difficult and resistant staff. Retrieved July 20, 2015, from http://www.naesp.org/principal-archives

Eller, J. F., & Eller, S. A. (2013, April). Working with difficult staff. *The Principalship, 70*(7). Retrieved July 20, 2015, from http://www.ascd.org/publications/educational-leadership/apr13/vol70/num07/Working-with-Difficult-Staff.aspx

Evans, R. (1996). *The human side of school change: Reform, resistance, and the real-life problems of innovation.* San Francisco, CA: Jossey-Bass, Inc.

Hanson, E. M. (1996). *Educational administration and organizational behavior.* Boston, MA: Allyn and Bacon.

Henderson, A. T., & Mapp, K. L. (2002). *A new wave of evidence: The impact of school, family, and community connections on student achievement*. Austin, TX: Southwest Educational Development Laboratory.

Houghton, S., Wheldall, K., & Merret, F. (1988). Classroom behavior problems which secondary school teachers say they find most troublesome. *British Educational Research Journal, 14*, 297–312.

Jackson, M. A., Perolini, C. M., Fietzer, A. W. Altschuler, E., Woerner, S., & Hashimoto, N. (2011). Career-related success-learning experiences of academically underachieving urban middle school students. *Counseling Psychologist, 39*(7), 1024–1060.

Johnson, S. M., & Kardos, S. M. (2000). Reform, bargaining and its promises for school improvement. In T. Loveless (Ed.), *Conflicting missions? Teachers unions and educational reform* (pp. 7–46). Washington, DC: Brookings Institution Press.

Kowalski, T. J. (1982). Organizational climate, conflict, and collective bargaining. *Contemporary Education, 54*(1), 27–31.

Lannie, A. L., & McCurdy, B. L. (2007). Preventing disruptive behavior in the urban classroom: Effects of the good behavior game on students and teacher behavior. *Education and Treatment of Children, 30*(1), 85–98.

Leithwood, K. A., & Riehl, C. (2003). *What we know about successful school leadership*. Philadelphia, PA: Laboratory for Student Success, Temple University.

McEwan, E. K. (2005). *How to deal with teachers who are angry, troubled, exhausted, or just plain confused*. Thousand Oaks, CA: Corwin Press.

Orloff, J. (2014). *The ecstasy of surrender: 12 surprising ways letting go can empower your life*. New York: Harmony Books.

Rick, T. (2011). *Top 12 reasons why people resist change*. Retrieved July 28, 2015, from https://www.torbenrick.eu/blog/change-management/12-reasons-why-people-resist-change/

Roe, T. M. (2006). *Union power and the education of children*. Stanford, CA: Hoover Institution.

Superfine, B. M., & Gottlieb, J. J. (2014). Teacher evaluation and collective bargaining: The new frontier of civil rights. *Michigan State Law Review, 3*, 737–788.

Tanner, R. (2015). *Organizational change: 8 reasons why people resist change*. Retrieved July 28, 2015, from https://managementisajourney.com/organizational-change-8-reasons-why-people-resist-change/

Van der Doef, M., & Maes, S. (2002). Teacher-specific quality of work versus general quality of work assessment: A comparison of their validity regarding burnout, psychosomatic well-being and job satisfaction. *Anxiety Stress and Coping, 15*, 327–344.

Van Voorhis, F. (2001). Interactive science homework: An experiment in home and school connection. *NAASP Bulletin, 85*(627), 20–32. Retrieved July 15, 2015, from http://www.sagepub.com/kgrantstudy/articles/10/van%20Voorhis.pdf

Walker, H. M., Ramsey, E., & Gresham, F. M. (2003/2004). Heading off disruption: How early intervention can reduce defiant behavior and win back teaching time. *American Educator*, Winter, 6–21.

About the Author

Dr. Vernon G. Smith is a professional educator and has served in the Indiana House of Representatives since 1990. Smith, a lifelong resident of Gary, previously served as Fourth District Gary City Councilman from 1972 to 1990.

He has severed as chairman of the Indiana Black Legislative Caucus and is the ranking minority member of the Indiana House of Representatives Education Committee. Additionally, Smith is a member of the Local Government and Judiciary Committees. Among Smith's top legislative achievements were sponsorship of the Indiana Commission on the Social Status of Black Males, creation of the Indiana Ombudsman Bureau, and authoring legislation awarding good time credit to inmates who get an education.

Currently serving as a professor of education at Indiana University Northwest, he is the coordinator of the Educational Leadership Program. He has served as interim dean for the School of Education. Smith's professional background includes experience at several public schools in Gary. He was the principal of Williams School from 1985 to 1992, principal of Nobel School from 1978 to 1985, and assistant principal of Ivanhoe School from 1972 to 1978. Smith taught in the Gary Public Schools System between 1966 and 1971.

His own educational background includes a BS degree from Indiana University, an MS degree from Indiana University, an EdD degree from Indiana University Bloomington, and post-doctorate studies at Indiana University Bloomington and Purdue University.

Active in several professional and civic organizations, Smith contributes his efforts to the work of the following groups: the Northern Indiana Association of Black School Educators, the Gary Association of School Administrators, the National Association for the Advancement of Colored People, the

Indiana University Alumni Association, the Northwest Indiana Urban League Board of Directors, and the Phi Delta Kappa Fraternity. He is a charter member of the Alpha Kappa Kappa Chapter of the Omega Psi Phi Fraternity, Inc.

Smith also helped found several civic groups, including the African American Achievers Youth Corps, Inc.; the Northern Indiana Association of Black School Educators; the Indiana City-Wide Festival Committee; the Young Citizens' League; the Vernon Stars; I.U. Dons, Inc.; and I.U. Gents, Inc.

Smith is the recipient of over 200 awards and honors, including the NAACP's Ovington Award, Gary Frontiers' Marcher's Award, the 2007 Hoosier Idol Award, the I.U. Northwest Alumni Association Division of Education Distinguished Educator Award, the Indiana Association of Chiefs of Police Appreciation Award, the Methodist Hospital Child and Adolescent Program Appreciation Award, the Brothers Keeper Appreciation Award, and the Indiana Association of Elementary and Middle School Principals Service Award.

Smith co-wrote *Building Bridges Instead of Walls: A History of I.U. Dons, Inc.* and authored *The Power of the Tongue* and *Against All Odds*. He has also written numerous magazine and refereed journal articles. His area of research is focused on the achievement and plight of African American males.

www.ingramcontent.com/pod-product-compliance
Lightning Source LLC
Chambersburg PA
CBHW030142240426
43672CB00005B/226